"What I love about Clapp's book *New Creation* is that he succinctly brings together a host of fellow travelers in dialogue with all of Scripture to dispel any notions that eschatology is merely about what happens in the end. In fact, what makes this book essential for disciples of Jesus is what Clapp does to help us see the implications of eschatology for our lives *now* in everything from sex to politics, climate change to Black Lives Matter, and all else that has to do with contemporary life. He accomplishes what he sets out to do—to demonstrate that eschatology is the key to understanding the biblical story into which we have been baptized."

—Dennis Okholm
Azusa Pacific University, Author of *Learning Theology through the Church's Worship*

"Rodney Clapp has done it again. He has paired a rigorous Eschatological Imagination with the ambiguities of apocalyptic times. His insistence on humans being story manufacturers who are desperate to experience and interpret those stories is not a new revelation, but his amplification of the critical importance of narrative is noted and appreciated. Combining insights from popular culture, Scripture, Church History, with a Pacifist Kingdom Theology, Clapp issues a primer that instructs and inspires. More than a standard operating primer, he has proposed a 'guide for the perplexed' and a 'manifesto' for flourishing in manically disturbed times. As one who has recently been through 'the valley of the shadow of death,' I found reading *New Creation* a witness to the Good News generating life in the ruins and signposts in a strange land (Walker Percy). This is theological reflection that is both richly informed and eminently accessible."

—Scott Young
Wesley Foundation Ministries, San Diego

NEW CREATION

A Primer on Living
in the Time Between the Times

NEW CREATION

Rodney Clapp

CASCADE *Books* • Eugene, Oregon

NEW CREATION
A Primer on Living in the Time Between the Times

Cascade Books
An Imprint of Wipf and Stock Publishers
199 W. 8th Ave., Suite 3
Eugene, OR 97401

www.wipfandstock.com

PAPERBACK ISBN: 978-1-5326-3964-7
HARDCOVER ISBN: 978-1-5326-3965-4
EBOOK ISBN: 978-1-5326-3966-1

Cataloguing-in-Publication data:

Names: Clapp, Rodney, author.

Title: New creation : a primer on living in the time between the times / Rodney
Clapp.

Description: Eugene, OR : Cascade Books, 2018 | Includes bibliographical refer-
ences.

Identifiers: ISBN 978-1-5326-3964-7 (paperback) | ISBN 978-1-5326-3965-4
(hardcover) | ISBN 978-1-5326-3966-1 (ebook)

Subjects: LCSH: Eschatology.

Classification: BT823 .C52 2018 (paperback) | BT823 .C52 (ebook)

Manufactured in the U.S.A.   08/15/18

To Jon Stock, S.B., fellow traveler.

We are not marching to Zion because we think that by our own momentum we can get there. But that is still where we are going. We are marching to Zion because, when God lets down from heaven the New Jerusalem prepared for us, we want to be the kind of persons and the kind of community that will not feel strange there.

—John Howard Yoder, *The Original Revolution*

CONTENTS

INTRODUCTION

The end is in the beginning. The farmer sows with the expectation of harvest. The carpenter lays a foundation with the whole and complete house in mind. The woman conceives a child with birth as the prospect. The journey begins with a destination in sight, at least in the mind's eye. Every morning, we leave our beds because we have projects beckoning us. We are storied creatures, and everything happens because we lean toward endings. These endings are the goals, the pursuits, the destinies, the termination points that mark and animate our lives. Without endings we could never begin anything. We would lack plots and our lives would be without purpose, devoid of meaning.

No wonder, then, that we are fascinated by stories. We like to rehearse a multitude of beginnings and endings. Some we try on for size, determining if they fit or might even transform the nonfictional story-project that is our life. Currently our culture is obsessed with zombie stories. Zombies by the hundreds shamble across our movie and television screens. They populate the pages of bestselling books and figure prominently in video games. Why do these stories resonate so much that we seem unable to get enough of them? And what sense of ends or endings do they bear?

I have three theories, not necessarily mutually exclusive.

The first is that zombie stories speak to our concern and dread of overpopulation. In the premodern world people interacted with a handful of persons in a typical day. And they knew most of those persons well. By comparison, we interact every day, face-to-face with dozens of office mates, cashiers, food servers, pedestrians, and so forth. Many of these we will never see again, let alone know by name. Add to that social media and the circles of hundreds (even thousands) of "friends" or "followers," better or lesser known, that we encounter through voluminous posts or tweets. On television we see dozens more faces, many barely registered. Add to this the fact that we are informed that the world groans under the weight of levels of human population unprecedented in human history. Population levels strain food resources and pollute the skies and waters of our cities. And our actual and virtual interaction with so many people constantly reminds us of these daunting facts.

Almost in every waking moment, then, we sense that there are so many of us, and worry if the world can sustain us. Thus we feel overrun with people—like the mindless zombies, they come at us in overwhelming hordes. The zombie stories touch a nerve. And they touch a nerve related to overpopulation: the issue of immigration. Here we see a sense of an ending that the zombie stories offer. If we already feel overwhelmed, we may not welcome the influx of new citizens, especially if they seem different or "other" than us. Still they seem to come and keep coming, crossing borders in a flood. Like the zombie hordes, they can only be stopped by walls. So an ending offered us is that we keep the zombies/immigrants out by constructing walls. Zombie stories resonate with the fear of immigration and the mood of wall-building. Thus it was no accident that the immigrant-averse presidential candidate, Donald Trump, in 2016 found it especially effective to place ads with the demographic watching the enormously popular zombie program *The Walking Dead*.

My second theory has to do with consumer capitalism. Especially since the 1990s, consumerism has been unleashed in North America and across the world. While capitalism had formerly concentrated on production, it now focuses overbearingly on consumption. Without massive and daily consumption, the consumer capitalist economy would collapse. Accordingly, whereas the hunter-gatherer consumed 1,900 kcals per day from foraged and hunted food, the average modern Westerner consumes 196,000 kcals per day—mainly from coal, oil, and gas sources.

Moreover, the consumer capitalist economy schools us to consume not only natural resources, but everything else besides. Tourism and other experiences have been monetized and commodified. We consume astounding amounts of media. We have come to see populations not as citizens, but as consumers. We imagine ourselves no longer as patients of doctors, but as healthcare consumers. Those sitting under teachers in our colleges are treated not so much as students as education consumers. We establish friendship networks to advance our careers and enhance our earnings, and so we relate to friends as objects of our consumption. Once I bumped into an acquaintance and we fell into conversation. I asked him where he was now worshiping. He was in the process of changing churches. "You know," he said casually, "the average church has a shelf-life of only about three years." The end here is to become consumers of everything and everyone we encounter.

Yet with this ending we relate, uncomfortably, not with the heroes who struggle to survive and hold off zombies, but with the zombies themselves. Like the zombies, we consume everything in our paths. We are often not mindful consumers, but, again like the zombies, almost mindless and soulless in our relentless devouring. Perhaps we are less content with omni-consumption than first appears. Among other things, we know that nature cannot endlessly bear the load of modern Western levels of consumption. We also yearn to be something more than consumers—to be citizens, to be friends of creation, even to be Christians (or Muslims, or Jews, or Buddhists) first and foremost, with all that entails. In other words, we are not entirely at ease with our basic identity as consumers. The zombie stories help us grapple with this sense of dis-ease, and name our condition as more dire than we might like to imagine.

My third theory to explain the mad popularity of zombies concerns bodily resurrection. The Christian hope is that we will not simply die and send our souls to heaven, but that one day our bodies will be resurrected. Without that confident and grounded hope, as the Apostle Paul said, we Christians are "people most to be pitied" (1 Corinthians 15:19). But we live in a world of lessening, and less hearty, faith. I need not rehearse statistics about the rise of the "nones," or non-religious. We are all aware that many of our churches (I speak here of the West, not denying the increase of professing Christians in the global South) continue to lose numbers and falter. Meanwhile, the general cultural atmosphere is less aware of and embracing of the Christian story and knowledge. In this environment, the hope of bodily resurrection is either unknown or regarded as a fantasy. What zombie stories do, then, is parody bodily resurrection. Instead of resurrecting to a full and flourishing state, the zombies resurrect as rapacious, mindless monsters, literally rotting in their steps. The ending here presents as the bleakest of our three theories. What lies in store for humanity is nothing more than a desperate, hardscrabble attempt to survive, to hold out not *for* resurrection but *against* resurrection. The zombie stories in this case point to a dis-ease additional to those of overpopulation and consumerism. It is an even deeper dis-ease, questioning hesitantly and gingerly, like a tongue probing an aching tooth, what is our hope in a world that in some ways appears to be without God, adrift in the cosmos. Or, to put it bluntly, are we simply and finally rotting in our steps? Is there no more ultimate ending than this?

NAMING THE SENSE OF ENDINGS

If the zombie stories were all we had, our sense of an ending would be bleak indeed. But of course there are other stories, other endings, on offer. As I have said, we are storied creatures. We are about inhabiting the best stories we can imagine (or that have been given to us). We incline toward stories that grant us an ending worth the investment of lives, of all our hopes and energies. This inclination for an ending proliferates in religions, mythologies, politics, and economics. In fact, the yearning for an ending is so strong and prevalent that the Christian tradition has a name for it.

Introduction

That name is eschatology. The word *eschatology* derives from the Greek *eschatos,* or "last." In Christian theology, eschatology encompasses the last times, what happens after death and at the end of history. It is a big word. But we need a big word to include everything under its purview, so to *eschatology* we resort.

The subject of this book is biblical eschatology, but before we turn directly to that, it is worth emphasizing that we live in a world of competing endings, or competing eschatologies. Besides the many fictional eschatologies available, like zombie stories, there are plenty of real-world eschatologies afoot.

For instance, following the fall of the Soviet Union in the late 1980s, and America's becoming the world's sole remaining superpower, some proposed that we had arrived at the end of history. Now capitalism and democracy would reign, alone supreme, and any subsequent time would devolve only from their perfection and unpacking. Since then, much has happened, and history has resumed in the dark light of extremist Islamic terrorism. But still some may imagine that the end—in terms both of history's goal and its terminus—lies in the United States' dominance and eventual victory over the entire world and all competing ideologies.

This is far from an entirely benign vision, but for sheer malignancy it does not match the regnant eschatologies of the bloody twentieth century. I speak of Stalin's Russia, Hitler's Third Reich (significantly called by its proponents, in millennial language, the "thousand-year Reich"), and Mao Zedong's communist China. Between them, these eschatologies, these attempts to see history to its close, resulted in millions upon millions of murders. Thus eschatologies can be dangerous, the lust for an ending a deadly thing.

We might speak of these eschatologies, including the (comparatively) more benign American version, as *presumptive eschatologies.* With self-will and an unwillingness to leave endings in God's hands, they grasp prematurely and arrogantly at bringing history to its peak. As we will see, Christianity itself can be guilty of presumptive eschatology. Part of living well in these last times, or the time between the times of Christ's two comings, is being able to discern a healthy, properly humble eschatology from a presumptive eschatology.

There is, finally, one other eschatology that bears mentioning. Observational science, unlike politics, does not try to bend history to its will. It simply looks at what is, and from such observation can predict the course of the universe. The picture is not pretty. In five billion years' time, the astronomers and cosmologists tell us, the Sun will deplete its hydrogen fuel and will swell enormously and burn up Mercury, Venus, and Earth.

The scientific hope, left solely to itself, is that humans by then will have traveled to and inhabited planets outside our solar system. But even if that is so, it is for humanity a temporary (if very long-lasting) reprieve. The universe is now 13.7 billion years old. When the universe is 10^{12} years old, stars will cease to form because there will be no hydrogen left, and all massive stars will have turned into neutron stars and black holes. By 10^{14} years, the universe will be a cold, utterly lifeless expanse composed of dead stars and black holes. Thus, as the Nobel Prize-winning physicist Steven Weinberg remarked, "The more the universe seems comprehensible, the more it also seems pointless." Ultimately, all that science can promise, strictly speaking, is futility.

Lethal presumptive eschatologies and the cold comfort of science make robust biblical eschatology all the more precious. For what biblical eschatology presents is an ending everlasting with God all in all, a cosmos comprised of peace and harmony—and not just a new heaven but a new earth, populated not only by humans at their flourishing best, but by (transformed) rocks and trees, dogs and bees. It points to a creation wonderfully made and yet more wonderfully restored. What's more, by biblical account that glorious ending has already begun in Christ.

I conclude these introductory remarks with a brief reading guide to this book. Chapter 1, the foundational chapter of the book, sets out the span of the biblical story with an eye to eschatology. Subsequent chapters will build on and reflect back to chapter 1, on the story of all stories. Chapter 2, on heaven and the resurrection body, puts heaven in its place as a way station but not our final destination. Chapters 3 through 5 explore three hallmarks of the eschatological people: priesthood, peace, and prayer. Chapter 6 then builds on a central affirmation of the first chapter, considering the place of non-human creation and human works in a restored cosmos. Chapter 7 returns to themes in chapter 2, about the resurrection body, and asks whether or not that body will include sexual identity and expression. Chapter 8 takes into account the crucial eschatological reality of judgment and what that may entail. Finally, the concluding chapter 9 considers the attitude or deportment granted to us for living as an eschatological people, a people of priesthood, peace, and prayer.

Chapter 1

THE STORY

<u></u>

Imagine you discover a discarded suitcase in your backyard. In the suitcase nestle sixty-six boxes, of various shapes and sizes. To make sense of the boxes, you must open them and examine their contents. But they are locked. Further unpacking the suitcase, you discover a key that will unlock the boxes.

The Bible, I want to suggest, is like this suitcase. Actually a library, the Bible is comprised of sixty-six books, written over a period of 1,500 years. The books represent a dazzling variety of genres: history, legend, love songs (The Song of Solomon), song and prayer books (the Psalms), wisdom literature (Proverbs, Ecclesiastes), prophecy, letters of exhortation, and outright end-of-the-world tracts (Daniel, Revelation). As anyone who has read (or tried to read) it from cover to cover can attest, the Bible is often confusing and difficult. Indeed, it resembles a vast and challenging nonfiction novel. To read it and make sense of it as a whole, we need a key.

That key is eschatology. What binds the Bible together, from beginning to conclusion, is the hope of an ending. In this chapter, then, I will review the biblical story with the eschatological key ready to hand. I will not, of course, offer an exhaustive review or reading—that would require several books. Instead, to depart from the key metaphor, I will range across the sacred library using an eschatological lens, looking at how the sense of an ending pervades and unifies the parts into a whole, into a single all-encompassing story. This story includes the purpose and God-intended ends not just of individuals, but of history and the entire cosmos. So the content itself excites and stimulates. Even more exciting is to know that we are invited to be inducted into this story, to become not merely readers of it but vital characters within it.

CREATION

"In the beginning . . . God created the heavens and the earth . . ." (Genesis 1:1). The Bible's first sentence is comprehensive. God creates all that is; the heavens and the earth comprehend the universe. The creation story proceeds in a series of permissives and commendations: "Let there be . . ." and "God saw that it was good . . ." First, "Let there be light," and "God saw that the light was good." Then, let there be a sky. Next, earth and the seas. "And God saw that it was good." Then, vegetation: "plants yielding seed, and trees of every kind bearing fruit with seeds in it." Again, "God saw that it was good." Next, the sun and the moon and the stars. "And God saw that it was good." Then, "swarms of living creatures" in the water, and in the sky "every winged bird of every kind." Again, "God saw that it was good." Next, God made the wild animals of the earth of every kind, and the domesticated animals ("cattle") of every kind. "And God saw that it was good." Finally, God created humankind in his image, "in the image of God he created them, male and female he created them." God surveys his completed creation, teeming with life of all sorts. "God saw everything he had made, and indeed, it was very good" (Genesis 1:4–31).

To appreciate the gentleness and evocativeness of the Genesis creation story, we can contrast it with the Babylonian epic of creation, contemporary to it. In the Babylonian epic of creation, the story centers on the ocean goddess Tiamat and the young warrior god Marduk. This creation begins with violent rebellion. Tiamat is an older goddess, and Marduk is the younger god appointed to overthrow her. In a gory frenzy, Marduk shoots her full of arrows, flays her, and stabs her heart. He tramples her corpse, crushes her skull, and scatters her blood in the wind—all to the cheers of the other younger gods. Finally Marduk splits Tiamat in two. From one half of her he makes the rain-bearing heavens. From the other half he makes the earth with its land, as well as springs, rivers, and oceans. Humanity is created as slaves of the gods, digging canals, cultivating crops, harvesting and preparing food for the gods, and, not entirely coincidentally, for the kings and priests who represent the gods. Slaughter and enslavement lie at the heart of this creation myth.

If the Babylonian epic presents the gods creating like blood-thirsty warriors, the Genesis story presents God creating like a loving artist, enthralled by his creation. God simply and gently speaks creation into being. We could say he delights it into being. In its repetition, rhythmic quality, and sense of celebration, Genesis 1 resembles nothing so much as a children's play chant or song. God gives creation a life of its own, permitting it to come alongside him and join him in the joyous chorus of life. So the "greater and lesser lights," the sun and the moon, are charged to govern or rule day and night (Genesis 1:16, 18). "The earth brought forth vegetation," cooperating with God in creation (Genesis 1:12). And the living creatures, including humankind, are called to "be fruitful and multiply," to fill and complete the creation of the waters and the land (Genesis 1:11–12, 20, 24). Generosity and freedom are at the heart of this creation story.

Note, now, the role of humanity in creation. Humanity is made in the image of God. This means humanity, at the crown of creation, is to "have dominion over the fish of the sea, and over all the cattle, and over all the wild animals of the earth, and over every creeping thing that creeps upon the earth" (Genesis 1:26). Humanity is made God's vice-regents or stewards on the earth. In God's image and after the way of God's artistry, humanity's "dominion" is not to be rapacious and exploitative. Instead, its stewardship is an exercise of generous and noncoercive power. Like God's power, this stewardly power invites, evokes, and permits. It is more power *with* and power *for* than power *over* the rest of creation. It is not

reflected in strip-mining, for example, which gouges off moun-
taintops, regarding trees and rocks only as much "overburden."
Nor is this stewardly power reflected when industries heedlessly
dump pollution into rivers or belch it into the skies. This power is
better reflected in the woodworker who brings out wood's natural
strength and beauty. It is reflected in the cook's seasoning and careful preparation that releases the glories of apples or green beans. It
is reflected in the vintner who patiently plants, prunes, cultivates,
and waters to evoke the grape's striking piquancy.

Such was the beauty and arrangement of creation. Set on this
trajectory, its end would have been progressive development beside and under humanity's benevolent stewardship. But then, as we
are all too aware, something went horribly awry.

FALL

Another, complementary account of the creation also gives us the
story of what is classically called the fall. God situates nascent humanity, Adam and Eve, in the Garden of Eden. They are at peace
with all the animals, whom Adam knows so well that he can name
them according to their essences. They have abundant fruit and
vegetation from which to eat, without toil. But they are commanded never to eat from the Tree of the Knowledge of Good and Evil.

They cannot bear this temptation and, seduced by the
smooth-talking serpent, they eat from the forbidden Tree. This
act results in a series of breaks or separations. First, humanity is
separated from God. Ashamed in their sin, they hide from God
and attempt to avoid his presence (Genesis 3:8). Second, they are
separated from one another. Confronted by God about the consumption of the forbidden fruit, Adam blames Eve, alienating
the two of them from one another (Genesis 3:12). Third, they are
separated from their fellow creation. Eve blames an animal, the
serpent, for her sin. And Adam is told that as a result of his sin the
food of soil and vegetation will no longer be easily available but,
with him alienated from it, will only produce fruit burdensomely,
with sweat and toil (Genesis 3:18–19). These three breaks provide

a deft working definition of sin. Sin is alienation from God, from others, and from creation.

These alienations go to the core of humanity. From them arises the first murder, Cain's killing of his brother Abel (Genesis 4:1–16). Murder is the worst of humanity's separation from God, from one another, and from the rest of creation. Within generations it becomes prevalent and because "the earth is filled with violence," God almost totally despairs of his creation (Genesis 6:13). Thus the end, the eschatology, of all creation almost comes to a premature conclusion. But from a worldwide flood sent to wipe the slate of creation clean, God rescues one righteous man, Noah, and his family (as well as an ark full of animals).

And after the flood God seems chastened. He establishes a covenant with Noah that he will never again destroy the earth by a flood and makes the rainbow the sign of this covenant. "When the bow is in the clouds, I will see it and remember my everlasting covenant between God and every living creature of all flesh that is on the earth" (Genesis 9:16).

That God will never totally despair of his creation and destroy it is good news. But still, sin remains, with all its mundane and horrific consequences. So there is a quandary. How to affirm creation, never give up on it, and yet also address sin and its catastrophic effects?

THE ELECTION AND MISSION OF ISRAEL

Notice through all of this that creation and, now the question of its rescue, is a universal concern. That is, creation and fall and the question of rescue have to do not with God and the individual (at least not first and foremost), but with God and all of God's creation. Too many readings of the Bible, and too many hymns and praise songs, make it sound as if creation and salvation are primarily about God relating to individuals, and only human individuals at that. But God's concern is bigger than that. God's concern is social, historical, political, and even cosmic.

We might think that God should have been done with it in his flood and scrubbed out all of creation. After all, not long after getting off the boat, Noah and his family themselves slip into grievous sin (Genesis 9:18–27). So why not wipe it all out and start with a clean slate? And this time, make humanity in such a way that it could not sin?

Because God wants a creation that can relate to him in freedom. Unlike the gods of the Babylonian epic, God does not want mere human slaves or automatons. For all the Babylonians expected, the gods could simply crack the whips louder. After all, terrorized slaves—from this brutal perspective—make the best, most compliant slaves. But God wants creation free because God wants creation to respond to him and to itself with love. Terror, or sheer overpowering, can produce relations of compliance. It can produce fearful obedience. But it cannot produce love, which by its very nature must be uncoerced. The rapist threatens death and gains compliance. The true lover seeks something much harder— and infinitely more satisfying—to attain. And God is a true lover.

So God is willing to take the long way around, to work with and in history—and history is about particulars. Thus to reclaim his free creation, God elects, or chooses, a particular people. He calls Abraham: "I will make of you a great nation, and I will bless you, and make your name great, so that you will be a blessing . . . And in you all the families of the earth shall be blessed" (Genesis 12:2–3). Abraham and Sarah, against all odds (they are old and Sarah has been barren), birth a son, Isaac. Isaac, with his wife Rebekah, bears Esau and Jacob. Jacob has another name, Israel, so directly from him comes the people Israel. Israel means "God-wrestler," and it is the nation God elects to wrestle with through history, so that "all the families of the earth shall be blessed." Thus begins a new eschatology, an ending toward which Israel will be the vehicle and conveyor.

All too soon, Israel is enslaved by Egypt. The Israelites cry out to the God of their fathers, that God may not forget them, and that God may liberate them from the Egyptians. And God does liberate them in the great event of the exodus, when Moses confronts the Pharaoh and eventually leads the Israelites through the Red Sea. At Mount Sinai, God delivers to Moses the Ten Commandments and the law by which Israel is to form itself as the nation of the true (and only) God. "Indeed," says God, "the whole earth is mine, but you shall be for me a priestly kingdom and a holy nation" (Exodus 19:5–6). Now, as a priestly kingdom, Israel will mediate to the world what it means to be a true, God-following and God-ordained people. As a holy nation, Israel is sanctified or set apart to reflect the world as the world is meant to be, responsive and responsible to the creator and redeemer God. This is what it means for Israel to be a light to all the nations of the world, that God's "salvation may reach to the end of the earth" (Isaiah 49:6; see also 42:6 and 60:3).

The Jewish political scientist Gordon Lafer unpacks this when he observes that the Jewish

> understanding of social solidarity helps make sense of the concept of a "chosen people," which will be a "light unto the nations." The example Jewish law seeks to set is one aimed not at individuals but specifically at other "nations." The institutions of solidarity that mark off Jews' commitments to one another from their more minimal obligation to outsiders are not designed to be applied as universal law governing all people, but rather to be reiterated within each particular nation. This, then, is the universalistic mission of Judaism: not to be a "light unto all individuals," not to establish an international system of justice, but rather to teach specific nations how to live *as* a nation.

This is no place to attempt to summarize Israel's national law and way of life. But one feature of it calls for comment. Israel, in its foundational story, has been freed from slavery and recognizes that its God is a God of justice and equity. So Israel has an abiding concern for the powerless and marginalized. Liberation theologians rightly speak of God's "preferential option for the poor." The theme of care and justice for the poor runs like a roaring river throughout the Old Testament, but I will here simply cite three representative texts:

> For he [God] delivers the needy when they call,
>> the poor and those who have no helper.
> He has pity on the weak and the needy,
>> and saves the lives of the needy.
> From oppression and violence he redeems their life;
>> and precious is their blood in his sight. (Psalm 72:12–14)

> Wash yourselves; make yourselves clean;
>> remove the evil of your doings from before my eyes;
> cease to do evil,
>> learn to do good;
> seek justice,
>> rescue the oppressed,
> defend the orphan,
>> plead for the widow. (Isaiah 1:16–17)

> He has told you, O mortal, what is good;
>> and what does the LORD require of you
> but to do justice, and to love kindness,
>> and to walk humbly with your God? (Micah 6:8)

Since it plays prominently in developing eschatology, I should mention here one other factor, or person, who figures importantly in Israel's political history. That is King David. He is Israel's greatest king, who united the twelve northern and southern tribes into a single confederation, and who established Jerusalem as Israel's capital. This gifted king was also a genius musician and poet, writing, most famously, Psalm 23 ("The Lord is my shepherd, I shall not want . . ."). David himself was capable of shocking sins, including the rape of Bathsheba and the murder of her husband, Uriah. Despite David's sins, God was able to work significantly through and with him. Thus Israel will come to hope for a great king and messiah (an "anointed one") in the wake and way of King David.

But it is not easy being the chosen people. Israel's history crests and craters, careens from faithfulness to apostasy, then repeats. Because of its sins, and because empires always loom, Israel is cast into exile. Even when the people is able to dwell in its land, it suffers from a succession of imperial overlords, from the Assyrians to the Babylonians to the Persians to the Greeks and, finally, to the Romans. So it still suffers a sort of exile. Israel yearns for independence and for full control of its homeland. In the midst of this vexing situation, prophets arise and call Israel back to her true mission and identity.

With the prophets abides a deep and urgent faith. God will not forget his covenant with Abraham and Israel. Eschatology develops. The prophets look ahead to a future when God will again hear Israel's cry, and act climactically to restore all of creation. The prophet Isaiah foresees a time when a Davidic, messianic figure will arise, then, wonderfully, justice will be done for the poor and the entire creation will be transformed into a state of peaceableness.

> A shoot will come out from the stump of Jesse [David's father],
>   and a branch shall grow out of his roots.
> The spirit of the LORD shall rest on him,
>   the spirit of wisdom and understanding,
>   the spirit of counsel and might,
>   the spirit of knowledge and the fear of the LORD.
>   . . .
> He shall not judge by what his eyes see,
>   or decide by what his ears hear;
> but with righteousness he shall judge the poor,
>   and decide with equity for the meek of the earth;
>   . . .
> The wolf shall live with the lamb,
>   the leopard shall lie down with the kid,
> the calf and the lion and the fatling together,
>   and a little child shall lead them.
> The cow and the bear shall graze,

their young shall lie down together;
  and the lion shall eat straw like the ox.
The nursing child shall play over the hole of the asp,
  and the weaned child shall put its hand on the
    adder's den.
They will not hurt or destroy on all my holy mountain;
  for the earth will be full of the knowledge of the LORD
as the waters cover the seas. (Isaiah 11:1–9)

Isaiah proclaims God's promise that he will create nothing less than "new heavens and a new earth" (Isaiah 65:17). The healed earth will participate in the joy and praise of this new creation:

For you shall go out in joy,
  and be led back in peace;
the mountains and hills before you
  shall burst into song,
  and all the trees of the field shall clap their hands.
Instead of the thorn shall come the cypress;
  instead of the brier shall come up the myrtle;
and it shall be to the LORD for a memorial,
  for an everlasting sign that shall not be cut off.
    (Isaiah 55:12–13)

There will be an anointed one sent to "bring good news to the oppressed, to bind up the brokenhearted, to proclaim liberty to the captives, and release to the prisoners . . ." (Isaiah 61:1–2). And Israel will be saved from exile and shine in its true identity as a priestly nation: "Strangers shall stand and feed your flocks, foreigners shall till your land and dress your vines; but you shall be called priests of the LORD, you shall be named ministers of our God; you shall enjoy the wealth of the nations, and in their riches you shall glory" (Isaiah 61:5–6).

As the Old Testament draws to a close, this is the great eschatological hope—that a messiah will come to lead Israel out of exile, to restore it wholly to its role as the one true nation. With the messiah's arrival will come justice for the poor and a renewed, peaceable creation.

JESUS: ISRAEL IN MINIATURE

"An account of the genealogy of Jesus the Messiah, the son of David, the son of Abraham" (Matthew 1:1). So begins the Gospel of Matthew, encapsulating in a few words the identity of Jesus of Nazareth. Jesus is Israel's long-awaited messiah. He hails from the line of Abraham, who was promised to be the father of a nation that would bring blessings to all of the earth. And he is the son of King David, the prototype of the messiah. Just as Samuel anointed David king, Jesus is baptized and anointed by John the Baptist. Just as David's anointing is followed by his battle with Goliath, Jesus's anointing is followed by his confrontation with Satan in the wilderness. David returned from his victory over Goliath to be met with rapturous popular acclaim; likewise, Jesus exits the wilderness and is by greeted by acclaim in Nazareth. David later wandered the wilds with his followers at peril of his life; Jesus and his followers also itinerate, sometimes under threat of lethal violence. Thus arrives the prophetically hoped-for new reign like the glorious King David's (see Isaiah 9:1–9, Jeremiah 30:8–9, and Amos 9:11–15).

In this and in other ways, Jesus recapitulates the story of Israel. Like Israel, Jesus experienced an exodus (this time not from but to Egypt—Matthew 2:15). Like Israel, Jesus wanders and is fed in the desert. Like Israel, Jesus cares especially for the oppressed, the orphan, and widow. In a sense, Jesus not only recapitulates Israel but reconstitutes Israel: not since the invasion of Assyria in 734 BCE has Israel been twelve united tribes, and Jesus calls exactly twelve disciples, symbolizing a newly recombined Israel. Jesus also effectively ends Israel's exile. The prophets Jeremiah, Ezekiel, and Isaiah preached that Israel was exiled for her sins. Jesus comes healing and forgiving sins (controversially, because this was thought to be the prerogative of God). Jeremiah spoke of the forgiveness of Israel's sin as a sign of return from exile:

> I [God] am going to bring it recovery and healing; I will
> heal them and reveal to them abundance of prosperity
> and security. I will restore the fortunes of Judah and the
> fortunes of Israel, and rebuild them as they were at first.
> I will cleanse them from all the guilt of their sin against
> me, and I will forgive all guilt of their sin and rebellion
> against me. (Jeremiah 33:6–8)

Accordingly, as the biblical theologian N. T. Wright observes,
"Forgiveness of sins is another way of saying return from exile." Yet
there is more. Jesus not only encapsulates the story of Israel—is
Israel in miniature—but brings that story to its eschatological climax by declaring and embodying the kingdom of God.

THE KINGDOM OF GOD INAUGURATED

Jesus comes among common people, among peasants. He speaks
their language. His parables brim with allusions to their life and
work, with references to seeds sown, wheat and weeds, mustard
seeds, yeast in dough, the desperation of day laborers hoping for
a few hours of work. With such parables, suffused with mundane
materials, he illustrates the kingdom of God come and coming:
how it is planted and is mysteriously growing, how it leavens with
light the gloomy world surrounding it, how the little can become
great. And always his eye is on the little, the needy and the lost. He
says when you feed the hungry, clothe the naked, visit those sick
and in prison, what you do for the least of these, you do for me
(Matthew 25:31–45).

He embodies the kingdom of God by works of wonder, by
his healing and exorcisms. His healing not only sees to the good
of ill and injured individuals, but reincorporates them into full
standing in the community. Consider the case of the woman with
a hemorrhage (Mark 5:21–34). Her constant blood flow left her in
a state of perpetual impurity. She was literally untouchable, and
not allowed into the worship practices of the community. And so
she has been bereft and marginalized for twelve years. Then Jesus
passes through a crowd and she grasps the hem of his garment.

She is healed, both in the sense of being freed from her disease and being made fit to re-enter the community in full standing. Jesus's exorcisms likewise return the demon-possessed, shackled and wandering in cemeteries, to communal life. With such works Jesus embodies—makes real physically and socially—the kingdom of God. And so he announces the coming of the kingdom in himself. "[I]f it is by the finger of God that I cast out demons, the kingdom of God has come to you" (Luke 11:20).

With the kingdom of God, then, comes healing and the defeat of Satan. With it also comes the defeat of death. In the middle of a funeral, Jesus raises a widow's son to life (Luke 7:11–17). So, too, he raises his friend Lazarus from the dead (John 11:38–44). Jesus demonstrates power over disease, Satan, and death. There is more: he forgives sin and rescues Israel and Israelites from exile. (Remember, "Forgiveness of sins is another way of saying return from exile.") And there is yet more. Jesus signals that salvation for all of creation comes through the arrival of the kingdom of God.

> And when he got into the boat, his disciples followed him. A windstorm arose on the sea, so great that the boat was being swamped by the waves; but he was asleep. And they went and woke him up, saying, "Lord, save us! We are perishing!" And he said to them, "Why are you afraid, you of little faith?" Then he got up and rebuked the winds and the sea; and there was a dead calm. (Matthew 8:23–26)

In the biblical world, the sea and its terrifying tumults represented all-consuming chaos and the forces of destruction. But Jesus, the kingdom in person, tames even these dark and raging forces.

Taken together, then, forgiveness of sins means the healing of the trifold alienation—from God, from others, and from creation—that we noted in our account of the fall.

Jesus supremely confronts sin (with its alienating effects), disease, demonic powers, and the forces of chaos when he dies on a cross. Once more he identifies with the least amongst the people of the earth. Crucifixion was a form of execution reserved for slaves and supposed traitors, for the lowest of the low. Naked, sweaty, bloody, tortured, and abandoned, Jesus on the cross absorbed the worst violence the political, religious, and demonic powers could levy. Through the cross he overcame sin and its alienation of humanity from God, from one another, and from creation. Through the cross, he relativized and tamed political powers: "He disarmed the rulers and authorities and made a public example of them, triumphing over them in it" (Colossians 2:15).

So the crucifixion is the rift between the old age, when principalities and powers rule, and the new age over which Jesus reigns (1 Corinthians 15:25–27). Through Jesus's death, the saints have been "set free from the present evil age" (Galatians 1:4). Because the Messiah has died and risen from the dead, "the end of the ages has come" (1 Corinthians 10:11). Everything old has passed away and there is a new creation (2 Corinthians 5:17).

Throughout the story of the Bible, there is no more fundamental divide than that between the Jews and the Gentiles. We must imagine our most deeply opposed categories to adequately represent the signal and gaping chasm between the Jews and the Gentiles. Democrats versus Republicans, black versus white, heterosexual versus homosexual, the USA versus China or extremist Islamic terrorism—none of these are greater divides than that which once separated Jews and Gentiles. And yet, according to the Letter to the Ephesians, even that towering, impenetrable wall has been breached through Jesus's work on the cross.

> So then, remember that at one time you Gentiles by birth, called "the uncircumcision" by those who are called "the circumcision"—a physical circumcision made in the flesh by human hands—remember that you were at that time without Christ, being aliens from the commonwealth of Israel, and strangers to the covenants of promise, having no hope and without God in the world. But now in Christ Jesus you who were once far off have been brought near by the blood of Christ. For he is our peace; in his flesh he has made both groups into one and has broken down the dividing wall, that is, the hostility between us. He has abolished the law with its commandments and ordinances, that he might create in himself

> one new humanity in place of the two, thus making
> peace, and might reconcile both groups to God in one
> body through the cross, thus putting to death that hostil-
> ity through it. (Ephesians 2:11–16)

Tremendous and all-encompassing as it is, the work of the cross would have meant nothing without the resurrection. There were other messianic candidates in Jesus's world. There were others who were killed and whose names are lost in the fog of history. But Jesus's name was not forgotten. Jesus was raised from the dead. In raising Jesus from his ignominious death, God vindicated him as the true Messiah. He is the "firstborn from the dead," so that "through him God was pleased to reconcile to himself all things, whether on earth or in heaven." Indeed, in him "all things"—and I underscore that this means all things in the universe—"hold together" (Colossians 1:17–20).

THE KINGDOM YET TO COME

So the kingdom has come in Christ. The end of all things, in the sense of both a goal and a terminus, is upon us (1 Corinthians 10:11). And yet people get sick. People still die, whether tragically or peacefully in bed. Earthquakes, tsunamis, hurricanes, and tornadoes rage, and thousands perish. Children starve. Creation moans and chokes under the poisonous weight of carbon dioxide released into the atmosphere. Old wars flare, and new wars break out. Clearly all is not yet right with the world. What does this mean?

It means that the kingdom has been inaugurated in Christ, but has not yet come in its fullness. The decisive blow has been struck. Christ has defeated sin and death and evil on the cross and through the resurrection. We are invited to live now in light of the kingdom come. But we await the kingdom's consummation, its ultimate manifestation.

Inducted into the biblical story, we look ahead to Christ's return or *parousia*, when God will raise the dead into transformed, new bodies (1 Corinthians 15). God will judge and set right all wrongs, and then will come a new heaven and a new earth, free of violence, of death, of all that separates us from God, from one another, from creation itself. Thus the Apostle Peter anticipates Jesus's return, which will effect the "*universal restoration* that God announced long ago through the prophets" (Acts 3:21). And 2 Peter 3:13 similarly declares that, "in accordance with [God's] promise, we wait for new heavens and a new earth, where righteousness is at home." At the fullness of time, the Letter to the Ephesians says, God "will gather up all things in [Christ], things in heaven and things on earth" (Ephesians 1:10). At more length, the Apostle Paul writes:

> For the creation waits with eager longing for the revealing of the children of God; for the creation was subjected to futility, not of its own will but by the will of the one who subjected it, in hope that the creation itself will be set free from its bondage to decay and will obtain the freedom of the glory of the children of God. We know that the whole creation has been groaning in labor pains until now; and not only the creation, but we ourselves, who have the first fruits of the Spirit, groan inwardly while we wait for adoption, the redemption of our bodies. (Romans 8:19–23)

Paul is saying that creation itself—the rocks and trees, the dogs and bees—awaits a fulfillment and restoration. Now creation is subject to futility and decay. But when humanity is raised bodily, when the kingdom is manifest, then creation will be "set free." Remember our earlier discussion of the creation story in Genesis, with humanity being made in the image of God to steward creation and help creation realize its potential. Here Paul looks ahead to the fulfillment of that stewardly role, for the image of God to be realized without mitigation or the stain of sin. Then humanity will rightfully and beneficently rule over creation. Then creation will not choke and moan, but will breathe freely and praise fully. The "universal restoration" will be gloriously realized.

Lastly, I note the book of Revelation. In Revelation 21, the seer witnesses "a new heaven and a new earth" (v. 1), where the

New Jerusalem descends from heaven to earth. All tears and causes for tears are wiped away (v. 4). "Death will be no more" (v. 4). From the glorious, bejeweled city will flow a river nourishing trees of life, whose leaves "are for the healing of the nations" (22:2).

This creation-spanning redemption is what we look forward to. For now, we live in the time between the times. We live in the time between the inauguration and the fulfillment of the kingdom. An old metaphor helpfully expresses this situation. In World War II, the Allies strategically defeated the Axis powers at the so-called D-Day invasion. At that point the war was decided—though battles remained, it was only a matter of playing out the war to its now foreordained end, at V-Day. Similarly, in Christ's cross and resurrection, D-Day has occurred for the powers of darkness and disintegration. We await V-Day, or Christ's *parousia* or return, when finally all things in heaven and on earth will be made right.

The D-Day/V-Day metaphor works, however, only so long as we do not imagine the time between the times as an age of steady, uninterrupted progress. The time between the times is more complicated than that. It is marked by a blend of faithfulness and apostasy, of moves forward toward justice met with considerable setbacks, of renewal and disintegration. So progress in or toward the kingdom must be judged on a case-by-case basis. In the time between the times, we cannot expect that we or the world are gradually and consistently advancing toward the kingdom. For the arrival of the fullness and completeness of the kingdom, we are dependent on God's inbreaking, still-future power. Until then, we must be ever discerning about new injustices, or old injustices undetected or ignored. We live with profound hope, yet with realism and without sentimentality.

ESCHATOLOGICAL POLITICS

Here concludes my all-too-brief account of the eschatological story. Despite its brevity, I hope it indicates how thrillingly large and all-embracing the story is. It is so big, in fact, that in order to live in the light of this story we need a politics, a way of working and living faithfully as a people. Politics in this sense is the organization and negotiations of a people pursuing a common good. And, as we have seen, the common good in sight with the eschatological story encompasses nothing less than a new heaven and a new earth.

Not surprisingly, then, the eschatological story reverberates with a politics. The political motif shows up in a number of key themes. First is God's kingdom come and coming. *Kingdom* is obviously a political concept, involving the rule of a sovereign—in this case God. To work on behalf of this kingdom, to dream for its full rule, most definitely entails a politics.

Next is the *euangelion*, the evangel or good news that the kingdom is come and coming. In the Greco-Roman culture of the New Testament, *euangelion* referred to decidedly political news, such as the announcement brought by a runner that an important battle had been won, or that an heir was born to the king. The good news the eschatological story announces is that Christ the king, on his cross and through his resurrection, has won the most important battle of all, defeating sin, death, and evil. It would not be amiss to render our term Gospel as "political tidings," such that we might understand the first four books of the New Testament as "The Political Tidings According to Matthew, Mark, Luke, and John."

The evangel declares Christ as *kyrios,* or Lord. *Kyrios* is the identical term used by Roman emperors who were deified, said to have become themselves gods. So Christ the *kyrios* directly confronts the highest claims of the Roman emperor and, by extension, any other overweening governmental power, then or now. To confess, to pray to, Christ as Lord is to pledge our highest political allegiance.

Consider, too, our term *church,* for the body designated to proclaim and witness to the Lord of the kingdom come and coming. *Church* in the New Testament Greek is *ekklesia,* or those called out. In its original context it denoted a social and political body pursuing its common good. So we would not be amiss to render *ekklesia* as the "town hall of God" or the "congress of the kingdom-people."

NEW CREATION

Finally, the term *parousia* carries political connotations. It was used of an emperor or other dignitary visiting a vassal community. It could be rendered a "royal arrival," and was greeted with pomp and circumstance. Accordingly, Christians live now awaiting the Lord's royal arrival at the end of time.

In sum, the eschatology set out here, in our dash across the Bible, is both inaugurated and holistic. It is inaugurated in the sense that it points to the kingdom already come and yet still to come in its fullness. It is holistic in the sense that it includes all of creation. To serve this comprehensive eschatological kingdom in the time between the times requires not an individualistic gospel, but a full-blown politics. This means that the church does not so much *have* a politics as *is* a politics—a body of people pursuing no less a common good than the flourishing of all creation. "So if anyone is united to Christ, there is a new world; the old order has passed away, and a new order has already begun" (2 Corinthians 5:17 NEB).

Chapter 2

HEAVEN

My father died a young man. At the age of forty-three he was diagnosed with cancer. A year later, he was gone. As is its wont, the cancer ravaged his body, leaving him an emaciated, starved shell by the time of his death. At his funeral, the pastor preached on how Dad was now free of that devastated body, once and for all. His soul, liberated permanently from the body, had flown to heaven. There was no mention of the hope for a healed, renewed, resurrected body, let alone the new creation.

Too many funeral (and other) sermons are like this. When preachers preach this way they are better Platonists than Christians. Plato was the great Greek philosopher who has influenced all philosophers since. I do not mean to denigrate him. There is much in his legacy to admire, and early as well as medieval Christianity owes him a debt in its thought. Yet we as Christians should decisively depart from Plato's lead when it comes to the body and the soul. Plato saw the soul as weighed down and held back by the body, which contaminated and obscured the soul's apprehension of truth and goodness. Plato, through his teacher Socrates, could even speak of the body as the "prison house" of the soul. In sermons and popular reflections like those at my father's funeral, Plato still speaks today. Down through the centuries, he is the great ventriloquist who would have Christians focus on heaven as the final dwelling place of souls gratefully freed from their bodies.

But as I hope chapter 1 has shown, this grossly misconstrues the biblical story and the biblical hope. In fact, the Christian story triply sanctifies the body. First, the body is created and, as Genesis 1:31 has it, is part of the creation pronounced "very good." Second, the body is sanctified in Christ's incarnation. Jesus assumes and is a human body, without incurring sin. The incarnation blesses physical and material creation. Third, the body will be resurrected and glorified. <u>Resurrection means that God never gives up on the body.</u>

The Christian hope is for a new heaven and a new earth, for universal restoration, including the resurrection of our bodies. In this time between the times, the kingdom of God has come and is yet coming in its splendid, comprehensive manifestation. "For the grace of God has appeared, bringing salvation to all, . . . while we wait for the blessed hope and manifestation of the glory of our great God and Savior, Jesus Christ" (Titus 2:11–13).

But what about heaven? Where is my father now, having died before the *eschaton*, before the "manifestation of the glory of our great God and Savior, Jesus Christ"? Assuming you and I die before the *eschaton*, what will happen to us after death?

WHEN HEAVEN CAN'T WAIT

Though the overarching eschatological story is clear, and the new creation is our ultimate destination, there are a few texts that indicate those who die before the *eschaton* will rest with God and Christ in heaven. The most pointed are two statements from the Apostle Paul. In Philippians 1:21–24, he says, "For to me, living is Christ and dying is gain. If I am to live in the flesh, that means fruitful labor for me; and I do not know which I prefer. I am hard pressed between the two: my desire is to depart and be with Christ, for that is far better; but to remain in the flesh is more necessary for you." Paul appreciates his labors for the gospel in this life, and he wants to serve the living Philippians. But he yearns to be more directly with Christ, and appears to expect that would be immediately so if he were to die and depart this life. In the same vein, he writes in 2 Corinthians 5:8, "Yes, we do have confidence, and we would rather be away from the body and at home with the Lord." Where else to be immediately "at home with the Lord" except in heaven?

We may also note Revelation 7:9–10:

> After this I looked, and there was a great multitude that no one could count, from every nation, from all tribes and peoples and languages, standing before the throne and before the Lamb, robed in white, with palm branches in their hands. They cried out in a loud voice, saying, "Salvation belongs to our God who is seated on the throne, and to the Lamb!"

Here the seer gazes into heaven and witnesses a great multitude, waving palm branches and praising God and the Lamb (Jesus Christ). The language is poetic, but there does indeed appear to be a heaven, and a well and diversely populated one at that.

Finally there are two incidents from the Gospels. In one, at Luke 23:39–43, Jesus hangs on his cross between the crosses bearing two criminals. One criminal taunts Jesus. The other, however, protests his companion's abuse. We criminals, he says, have been "condemned justly" and "are getting what we deserve for our deeds, but this man has done nothing wrong." Then he requests, "Jesus, remember me when you come into your kingdom." And Jesus responds, "Truly I tell you, today you will be with me in paradise." *Today,* he says, not at the end of time, they will dwell in paradise, or heaven.

The other heavenly incident in the Gospels occurs at John 14:2, when Jesus tells the disciples, "In my Father's house there are many dwelling places. If it were not so, would I have told you that I go to prepare a place for you?" Here, the Greek for "dwelling places" indicates a temporary lodging. It is a way station for those dead before the *parousia* and the advent of the new creation. Resided in by God and Christ, and surely full of praise from its human residents, it is definitely pleasant and radiant. But it is not the final destination.

We are habitual creatures, and those used to the simple Christian story of individuals dying and going to heaven—the end—may feel insecure at talk of a new creation that may seem to rob them of heavenly hope. They need not be anxious. We can, and I do, affirm a heaven immediately after death. The point is not exactly that heaven is a wrong hope. It is that, by itself, heaven is a hope too small. It is as if someone started on a journey, seeking a great destination, but stopped and settled for a pleasant way station instead of pushing on to an even more marvelous and beautiful city. Imagine a pioneer sojourning west and wanting to live by a canyon. Upon reaching the Palo Duro Canyon in west Texas, she is struck by its glowing red hues and towering rocks, and stops and stays there because she cannot imagine a more magnificent canyon. But she has never seen the Grand Canyon! Simply put, heaven must be wonderful. Yet it is penultimate, not ultimate. It does not match the new creation, when heaven and earth are twinned, when we are reclothed in our transformed bodies, when heaven and the entire universe are shot through and shimmering with the glory of God.

I think there is a balance. It is struck by an Episcopal blessing often said at funerals. The people intone, "May she [the deceased] rest in peace and rise in glory." That is to say, may the dead now rest peacefully in heaven, but one day rise bodily in glory. May she, may all the dead in Christ, know God's delights today in heaven, and one day know them even more expansively and intensively in the new creation.

WHAT ABOUT THE RESURRECTION BODY?

What might our bodies be like in this expansive and intensive existence of the new creation? What, exactly, rises in glory?

One text in the New Testament addresses these questions squarely. It is the fifteenth chapter of Paul's First Letter to the Corinthians. There Paul compares the earthly, present-day body to the resurrected body by appealing to the metaphor of seeds and mature plants. The seed (the earthly body) is not identical to the plant (the resurrected body). An acorn does not resemble a grown oak. A sunflower seed looks starkly different from the gawky, bright yellow flower it grows into. Yet there is obviously continuity and some kind of identity between the seed and the mature plant. We cannot sow an acorn and expect a sunflower, or sow a sunflower seed and produce an oak tree.

Similarly, says Paul, there is continuing identity and yet contrast between the earthly and the resurrected body. "What is sown is perishable, what is raised is imperishable. It is sown in dishonor, it is raised in glory. It is sown in weakness, it is raised in power. It is sown a physical body, it is raised a spiritual body" (1 Corinthians 15:42–44). So the earthly body is perishable and corruptible, susceptible to death and decay. But the raised body is (by God's graceful empowerment) imperishable, incorruptible, and not susceptible to death. In a word, it is immortal.

You may notice that Paul's language for the resurrected body is the "spiritual body." At first glance, this appears an oxymoron to us. We think of the spiritual as immaterial and ethereal, exactly the opposite of the physical. So how can there be such a thing as a "spiritual body"? In the biblical texts, as theologian Anthony Thiselton points out, *spiritual* "nearly always denotes the quality of being animated, led, and sanctified by the Holy Spirit." So Paul's expression is not oxymoronic or self-contradictory. It simply indicates that the resurrected body is vivified, guided, and empowered by the Holy Spirit. The Holy Spirit makes the resurrection operative (Romans 8:11).

There is, then, identity and yet discontinuity between our physical, earthly bodies and our spiritual, resurrected bodies. We may make these similarities in difference more concrete, and elaborate on them, by referring to the stories of Jesus's resurrection appearances. He is, after all, the first-fruits of the resurrection, the alpha-man of the omega of our own resurrection, the A to the Z of our own spiritual bodies. So we may learn something by observing the properties and events of his resurrection body.

NEW CREATION

We may first notice that Jesus's resurrected, spiritual body was physical and material. It appears to the physical senses of the disciples and others who encountered it. It can be seen, heard, touched, and presumably smelled. The disciple Thomas, who was not present at Jesus's first appearance to the disciples, doubts that the Lord has been raised. He objects, "Unless I see the mark of the nails in his hands, and put my fingers in the mark of the nails and my hand in his side, I will not believe" (John 20:24). A week later Jesus appears again, and this time Thomas is on the scene. Jesus invites Thomas to touch him. Then, with the solidly material master standing before him, Thomas believes (John 20:27–28).

In addition, the resurrected Jesus consumes food. "They gave him a piece of broiled fish, and he took it and ate in their presence" (John 24:42–43). Later, he shares a campfire, seaside breakfast of fish and bread with seven disciples (John 21:9–11). So we may expect our resurrection bodies to be material and sensual. They will be capable of eating, and so we may share in the Lord's feast, as anticipated in Isaiah 25:6: "On this mountain the LORD of hosts will make for all peoples a feast of rich food, a feast of well-aged wines, of rich food filled with marrow, of well-aged wines strained clear." And in the words of Jesus himself: "Then people will come from east and west, from north and south, and will eat in the kingdom of God" (Luke 13:29; see also Matthew 8:11).

But while Jesus's resurrection body was clearly physical, it possessed unusual properties. It could somehow pass through and appear behind locked doors (John 20:19–26). In this regard, I am reminded of teleportation in the *Star Trek* television series, where bodies could be instantly "beamed" from one location to another. What we might then call "teleportation," the great Catholic theologian Thomas Aquinas referred to as "agility," saying that our resurrection bodies, like Jesus's, will be "prompt and apt" in their movements. With endless wonders to enjoy in the new creation, all suffused by the glory of God, we will be able to transit from place to place instantaneously.

There was something else. Jesus could be hard to recognize in his resurrection body. Mary Magdalene mistakes him for a

gardener beside the empty tomb (John 20:11:18). The two followers on the road to Emmaus walk a considerable distance with him,
and hear him expound the Bible at length, without yet recognizing
him (Luke 24:13–35). Peter and his six companions at the Tiberian
sea do not immediately recognize him when he asks them if they
have caught any fish (John 21:1–14). So somehow the resurrected
body looked different enough that, on occasion, even close friends
did not immediately recognize it.

Part of this may be accounted for by surprise. Mary and the
others knew Jesus had been killed. He was dead, and they were
not expecting to see him alive. I remember an occasion when I
was visiting my brother. He went to work one morning and I did
not expect to see him again before evening. But I had told him
that I was going to visit a bookstore. That afternoon while I was
browsing the shelves, I came across a man about my height, with
a graying crewcut and long fingers. I took no special account, but
then he greeted me: "Hi, Rod." Then I recognized this momentary
stranger as my brother, whom I have of course known all my life.
He had left work early and come looking for me. It was because I
did not expect him to appear in that time and place that I did not
at first recognize him.

Yet my non-recognition was only momentary, a matter of
seconds. Mary and the other disciples did not recognize Jesus for
minutes, and in the case of the followers on the road to Emmaus,
perhaps for an hour or more What, then, leads the surprised followers to recognize him when they do?

It is his reincorporation of them into his narrative, the story
of a life with him they had long experienced. For Mary, it comes
when he urgently calls her by name ("Mary!"). Then she cries,
"Rabbouni!" ("My master!" or "My teacher!"). He is no longer a
stranger, but the teacher she had long and intimately known. For
the Emmaus disciples, recognition comes when he blesses bread
and breaks it. Then they are again sharing a meal with their master,
as in the previous days of their story with him. For Peter and his
companions at the Sea of Tiberius, it comes when Jesus produces
a massive haul of fish, just as he had in former days fished with

them and multiplied a few pieces of fish and bread into a meal for thousands. Thus he reveals to them and continues his identity with them by resuming and restoring the narrative of their lives together. And ultimately this narrative is nothing less than the story of God at work in Christ and in their lives.

As the New Testament scholar Joel Green nicely puts it:

> Here is the move Jesus makes: He weaves a story; or rather, he picks up the story that is already present, the one in the Scriptures, within which, throughout his ministry, he has sought to inscribe himself. In an essential sense, his identity is lodged there, in the grand story of God. What is more, he shows that the Scriptures themselves can be read aright only with reference to him, only insofar as they are actualized in the continuity of his person from life to crucifixion and afterlife, in resurrection.

So, too, with us. Our resurrection bodies will not be absolutely identical with our present bodies, but we will be identifiable as ourselves in and as them. They will possess, by grace, remarkable abilities such as agility or teleportability. We will be recognizable as the same people who lived an earthly life, with our own unique histories. Most importantly, we will be recognizable because we too have been inscribed into the story of God, Jesus, and their Spirit. Our relationships, encompassing and granting our identity, will be resumed and restored within the grand biblical, eschatological story.

Put differently, we will be known first and last through our baptisms, for baptism gifts us with a new and most fundamental identity. Through baptism we die and are reborn into the kingdom and incorporated into the church, with all their social and political ramifications. Through baptism we are claimed as Christ's own. Through baptism we take on the new name—"Christian"—and are made a new creation. Through baptism we undertake the eschatological life. Through baptism we declare our ultimate allegiance, reordering all our ways of living under the banner of the cross.

In our resurrection bodies we will be known by our appearances, in a body resembling our old, earthly body. And yet, with new powers, we will be even more splendidly and truly ourselves. So, to say it again, we will resume and restore relationships. We will know the father and mother and sister who have gone on into death before us. We will reclaim them by the familiarity of their precious faces. But we will especially know them by their narrative incorporation in the most essential story of their lives, by their belonging to Christ as Lord of all lords. Then let the feasting begin.

Chapter 3

PRIESTHOOD

The New Testament's First Letter of Peter bristles with eschatology. At the start, we are told that Christ's resurrection has given us "new birth" and "an inheritance that is imperishable, undefiled, and unfading, kept in heaven for you, who are being protected by the power of God through faith for a salvation ready to be revealed in the last time" (1:3–5). In the same vein, the author notes that eschatological judgment is near to hand (1:12 and 4:5). In addition, the author writes early in the letter that Christ "revealed the end of the ages for your sake" (1:20), then similarly later: "the end of all things is near . . ." (4:7).

With his resurrection and ascension, Christ has moved to the right hand of the Father, where "angels, authorities, and powers [are] made subject to him" (3:22). The letter calls the beleaguered communities to which it is addressed to "rejoice insofar as you are sharing Christ's sufferings, so that you may also be glad and shout for joy when his glory is revealed," that is, when the kingdom is manifested in its fullness (4:13). When the "chief shepherd" appears at the climax of history, "you will win the crown of glory that never fades away" (5:4).

We see here how eschatology empowers. First Peter is written to exiles scattered across the better part of Asia Minor (1:1). These were displaced people, minorities removed from their homes and kin, people without full citizenship in their surrounding society. They suffered scorn as—in our contemporary language—refugees and immigrants.

And they suffered scorn as adherents of a "foreign religion," the Christianity that was derided as a faith for slaves. Their churches were little and seemingly insignificant, probably not consisting of more than a couple dozen people in each meeting. It is these overwhelmed and marginal people whom 1 Peter assures have an imperishable inheritance kept for them in heaven; that the Christ they worship is at the right hand of God, supreme over all powers heavenly and earthly; and that have crowns of glory awaiting them. The eschatological story conveys assurance and grants tremendous dignity. It is as if 1 Peter says, "You may appear to be little and inconsequential people, treated as disposables. But in reality you belong to the Lord of the universe, whose kingdom has come and is coming. You are a part of the story of nothing less than history's climax and the earth's remaking. Your station is high and exalted. Indeed, soon you will wear crowns."

ROYAL PRIESTHOOD

Soon they will wear crowns. But already they are royalty. To these bedraggled refugees and immigrants, 1 Peter declares, "But you are a chosen race, a royal priesthood, a holy nation, God's own people in order that you might proclaim the mighty acts of him who called you out of darkness into his marvelous light" (2:9–10). This text echoes Exodus 19:6, telling Israel: "you shall be for me a priestly kingdom and a holy nation." So our refugees and immigrants are inducted into the great story of Israel. They are now nothing less than a chosen race and a holy nation, a people among the peoples, a polity among the polities.

And they are a royal priesthood, conveying to the nations the message and acts of Christ, died and resurrected (1 Peter 1:3–5). Priests mediate. They stand between God and the community. They represent God to the community, and the community to God. And priests bless. They bless God on behalf of the world, and the world on the behalf of God. Now, says 1 Peter, the church—however small in numbers, however apparently insignificant its members—is a royal priesthood. Already the church's members are kings and queens. And, if we add the Apostle Paul's emphasis that Christians live and pray for the redemption of nature (Romans 8:18–30), they are kings and queens not just of the human world, but of all creation. As the biblical theologian Richard Middleton puts it, Christians are "priests of creation, actively mediating divine blessing to the nonhuman world and—in a post-fall situation—interceding on behalf of a groaning creation until that day when heaven and earth are redemptively transformed to fulfill God's purpose for justice and shalom [that is, peace, wholeness, cosmic well-being]."

If you are a Christian, this is your legacy. You are a member of a royal priesthood. You are called, amazingly, to stand at the center of the world and creation. You are called to represent the world to God, and God's ways to the world. Whatever your worldly station, you are a creature of enormous dignity. And with that dignity comes responsibility. The church as a royal priesthood is called not to abandon and denounce the world, however far astray it goes, however dark its violence and degradation, but to embrace the world and represent to it its own true dignity as a creature of God. Speaking of this priestly responsibility, the Eastern Orthodox theologian Alexander Schmemann writes, "If we do not stand precisely as representatives of this world, as indeed the world itself, if we do not bear the whole burden of *this* day, our 'piety' may still be pious, but it is not Christian."

What does priestly royalty look like on the ground? First Peter fills out the picture in detail. In a word, priestly royalty means to live as peacemakers. "May grace and peace be yours in abundance" (1:2). "Rid yourselves, therefore, of all malice and all guile, insincerity, envy, and all slander" (2:1). Ridden of malice and envy, all seeds of violence will be rooted out. "Conduct yourselves honorably among the Gentiles, so that, though they may malign you as evildoers, they may see your honorable deeds and glorify God when he comes to judge" (2:12). Here the concern is for the good of the Gentiles, even when they act spitefully, that finally they might see God in his royal priesthood and be saved from judgment. "Honor everyone. Love the family of believers. Fear God. Honor the emperor" (2:17). Only God deserves our ultimate reverence, or "fear." But act peaceably among the nations, so "Honor the emperor."

Most importantly, live within the church as the royal priesthood you are. Be in prevailing prayer to bless God and the world (4:7). "Above all, maintain constant love for one another, for love covers a multitude of sins" (4:8) Treat other believers as the kings and queens they are, with all the inestimable status that entails. Be they waitresses or CEOs, custodians or philanthropists, they are of equal and exalted value in the household of God. In this time between the times, no Christian body has exemplified this mutual respect more than the African-American church. Constantly slighted, subject to frequent abuse, African Americans found in the church a place where they could be and were treated with the human regard they were due. In church, however menial their day jobs might be, they stood tall and true. They built there a world of justice and dignity in a surrounding world of injustice and indignity.

First Peter continues, "Be hospitable to one another without complaining. Like good stewards of the manifold grace of God, serve one another with whatever gift each of you received" (4:9–10). Offer peace and food freely and joyously to one another. Serve the whole body with the gifts, the talents and spiritual resources, you have been given.

First Peter does not deny suffering, especially in this time between the times. We are not to be surprised that suffering and even persecution sometimes overtake us (4:12). If we suffer because of our commitment to Christ—if we are mocked for our witness, or lose a job promotion because we would not trample a work "competitor"—we can "rejoice insofar as [we] are sharing Christ's sufferings" and look ahead to the *eschaton* when Christ's glory will be revealed and we will "be glad and shout for joy" (4:13).

First Peter ends as it began, with the recognition of the peace that is ours in Christ, who through his cross broke down the dividing walls of suspicion between all people. "Peace," then, "to all of you who are in Christ" (5:14).

THE TEMPLE AND ESCHATOLOGY

In Israel, priests presided at the temple. The temple imagery richly suffuses and enriches the eschatological story.

It is hard to overstate the manifold importance of the temple and its rituals in pre-exilic Israel. We must remember that Israel had nothing like the modern separation of church and state. Nor did Israel have theaters or other media—its sole source for drama was the enacted rituals in the temple. Thus the temple bore mul-tilayered social, spiritual, economic, and cultural significance. In contemporary America it would be the equivalent of the entire range of our iconic political and cultural institutions: the White House, Capitol Hill, the National Cathedral, Wall Street, and Hollywood. More than this, Jerusalem, in a profound theological sense, was considered the center of the earth—the hill God would defend against all attackers. And at the center of Jerusalem was the temple, in whose innermost chamber, the holy of holies, the King of the Universe was known to dwell with an especially intense and awesome presence. To this temple's courts all the world would someday stream, bearing offerings and worshiping the earth's one true God (Psalm 96:8–10).

With this in mind, we return to the beginning, to Eden. In Genesis 1–2, Eden is presented as a sanctuary, a kind of temple where God dwells. Just as God met the priest within the holy of holies, God walked with Adam and Eve in the Garden (Genesis 3:8). Adam and Eve were priests, called to till God's Garden and keep his commands.

There are other parallels between Eden and the temple. The ark of the covenant was kept in the holy of holies. The ark contained the law, as a fount of wisdom, echoing the Tree of the Knowledge of Good and Evil, found in the center of the garden, which also led to (a hard-won) wisdom. Touching the ark, like touching the Tree, led to death. Also, both the entrance to Eden and the entrance to the temple faced east (Genesis 3:24 and Ezekiel 40:6). Finally, just outside Eden was a river bounded by land veined with gold, bdellium, and onyx (Genesis 2:12). Likewise, the sacred furniture in the temple was made of gold. Bdellium was a fragrant substance, looking like manna (Numbers 11:7), which was stored in the ark of the covenant. And onyx stones were abundant in the temple, especially on the breastplate of the high priest (Exodus 25:7; 28:9).

With such parallels, it is no wonder the prophet Ezekiel could refer to Eden as a temple (Ezekiel 28:13) and the psalmist could hymn, "They feast on the abundance of your house [temple], and you give them drink from the river of your delights [literally, Eden]" (Psalm 36:8).

Next, recall that Eden's paradise was originally intended to spread out and expand across the world. God called Adam not only to till the Garden but to "fill the earth" (Genesis 1:28) as a priestly steward. Of course, Adam failed. Had he not, the entire earth would have become a temple, open to God's intense and immediate presence. So for awhile the focus narrowed onto Jerusalem's temple. But the temple was associated with creation as it was supposed to be, without sin. In the meantime, prophets longed for the restoration of the Edenic temple, of a whole earth shot through with God's presence. Thus, Isaiah: God "will comfort all of her waste places, and will make her wilderness like Eden, her desert like the garden of the LORD" (Isaiah 51:3). And Ezekiel: "And they will say, 'This land that was desolate has become like the garden of Eden . . .'" (Ezekiel 36:35).

JESUS AND THE CHURCH AS TEMPLE

The waiting is over with the arrival of Jesus on the scene. Breathtakingly, Jesus took onto himself all the temple symbolism and imagery. He and his disciples walk in the city of Jerusalem, overshadowed by the massive presence of the temple. (It occupied about a quarter of the city's space.) There Jesus says that the temple will be destroyed and raised in three days. The Jews who hear him—deeply impressed with the magnificent temple and all it stands for—are incredulous. They say, "This temple has been under construction for forty-six years, and you will raise it in three days?" But, says the Gospel of John, "he was speaking of the temple of his body" (John 2:19–21). Jesus will be crucified and then, after three days, raised from the dead. The temple will stand in a new form, in the person of the Jew from Nazareth.

In the same vein, Jesus calls himself the cornerstone of the new temple. "Jesus said to them, 'Have you never read in the scriptures: 'The stone that the builders rejected has become the cornerstone; this was the LORD's doing, and it is amazing in our eyes'?" (Matthew 21:42, echoing Psalm 118:22–23). Many of the people will spurn him, but he is nothing less than the new cornerstone of the new temple. And just as forgiveness was asked and received in the temple, he operates as the temple in miniature and freely absolves people of their sin. Truly, as G. K. Beale and Mitchell Kim write, "To call Christ the 'temple' is merely another way of referring to him as the new creation, since the temple was symbolic of creation and the coming new cosmos."

But, as is often the way with eschatology, there is more. Incorporated into Christ's body, the church itself becomes the temple. Says the Apostle Paul to the Corinthian congregation, "Do you not know that you are God's temple and that God's Spirit dwells in you?" (1 Corinthians 3:16). And later he observes, "For we are the temple of the living God . . ." (2 Corinthians 6:16). First Peter exhorts, "like living stones, let yourselves be built into a spiritual house [that is, the temple] (1 Peter 2:5). The Letter to the Ephesians similarly notes that the church is "built together spiritually into a dwelling place for God" (Ephesians 2:22). Just as the temple was the special dwelling place for God, now the church is a new and eschatological temple.

The church as temple has a new high priest in Christ. "We have such a high priest, one who is seated at the right hand of the throne of Majesty in the heavens and the true tent [or tabernacle, the temple in its earliest form] that the Lord, and not any mortal, has set up" (Hebrews 8:1–2). God calls the church, this temple in the flesh, to witness and sacrifice on behalf of the nations. This sacrifice is not the sacrifice of animals' bodies, but the sacrifice of our praise and bodies, our whole lives. "Let mutual love continue. Do not neglect to show hospitality to strangers . . . Remember those in prison . . . [and] those who are being tortured . . . Let marriage be held in honor . . . Keep your lives free of the love of money . . ." (Hebrews 13:1–6). "I appeal to you therefore, brothers and sisters," the Apostle Paul writes, "by the mercies of God, to present your bodies as a living sacrifice, holy and acceptable to God, which is your spiritual worship" (Romans 12:1).

Through the sacrifice of praise and our bodies, through holy habits, we are made fit to occupy the new heaven and the new earth. The temple imagery continues to the end of the Bible. When the city of heaven descends to the earth, its streets will be paved with gold, just as gold was abundant in the temple's holy of holies (Revelation 21:18; see also 1 Kings 6:20–22). And the city (we are speaking symbolically here) will be a cube (Revelation 21:16), just as the holy of holies was a cube (1 Kings 6:20). The holy of holies, then, will expand to encompass the entire new creation. God will be especially, immediately, universally, and intensely present. Look before you: God. Look behind you: God. Look to your left: God. Look to your right: God. Look above and below: God. Look at others: God. Look to the rocks and trees, the dogs and bees: God. The whole earth will become a temple, filled with God and the praise of God.

LIVING AS A ROYAL PEOPLE IN THE TIME BETWEEN THE TIMES

The new creation in its fullness is yet to come. But today, right now, the church is a royal priesthood. When you worship with the church, you are surrounded on all sides by kings and queens. The Christian who stands before and beside you is royalty. You and they together possess an elite, incomparable status. And the non-Christian, the person outside the church who stands before and beside you, is a potential king or queen. As C. S. Lewis wrote in his greatest essay,

> There are no *ordinary* people. You have never talked to a
> mere mortal . . . But it is immortals whom we joke with,
> work with, marry, snub, and exploit . . . We must play.
> But our merriment must be of that kind (and it is in fact
> the merriest kind) which exists between people who
> have, from the outset, taken each other seriously—no
> flippancy, no superiority, no presumption.

Let there be merriment, then, and that abundantly. For
Christians will "be glad and shout for joy" (1 Peter 4:13). The eschatological people, leaning into the victory of the new creation,
have plenty about which to be merry. But always, deep and abiding
respect, the respect owed royalty.

To live in the time between the times also means to live in exile of a sort. "For here we have no lasting city, but we are looking for
the city that is to come" (Hebrews 13:14) First Peter is addressed
to exiles (1:1), who still find themselves under the sway of Rome,
which they call "Babylon" (5:13). Accordingly, in the time between
the times we do not expect or strive for a theocracy. Christians live
nonviolently and noncoercively (see chapter 4). We strive to dwell
peaceably and beneficently with our neighbors. We hope for their
good, for our own good will be realized with them. As the prophet
Jeremiah put it,

> Thus says the LORD of hosts, the God of Israel, to all the
> exiles whom I have sent into exile from Jerusalem to
> Babylon: Build houses and live in them; plant gardens
> and eat what they produce. Take wives and have sons
> and daughters; take wives for your sons, and give your
> daughters in marriage, that they may bear sons and
> daughters; multiply there, and do not decrease. But seek
> the welfare of the city where I have sent you into exile,
> and pray to the LORD on its behalf, for in its welfare you
> will find your welfare. (Jeremiah 29:4–7)

A proper eschatological perspective forswears lording over
the world. It does not expect any nation, however powerful or de-
cent, to be the church or to usurp the church's role as itself a "holy
nation" (1 Peter 2:9). Above all, then, the church keeps its own

house in order, for "judgment [will] begin with the household of God" (1 Peter 4:17). The church in its politics, in its pursuit of a common good, will be about tending to and honoring one another. It will witness to the world the possibilities of a true nation, one marked by mutual respect and justice and peace.

In this ambiguous time between the times, the church will approach politics outside its walls carefully. It will always keep God's kingdom come and coming in Christ alone uppermost in its vision. It will not mistake any party or government or movement, however praiseworthy, for the kingdom of God. But it will engage these politics boldly and confidently, and always with an eye to the powerless and easily forgotten or abused. If the Republicans are the last ones caring for the unborn, the Christian will be among them. If the Greens are the last fighting for a caring stewardship of creation, the Christian will be among them. If the Democratic Socialists are the last ones caring for the poor and the working class, the Christian will be among them. If Black Lives Matter are the last ones believing that black lives do matter, the Christian will be among them. If the relief agencies are the last ones caring for refugees, the Christian will be among them. If the pacifist anarchists are the last ones standing against war, the Christian will be among them.

Mutual respect, then, and merriment. A politics centered on the church's role as a holy nation and royal priesthood, but engaged with other politics selectively and always with a lesser allegiance. Such, wondrously, is life and witness in the time between the times.

Chapter 4

PEACE

A nyone who spends time on the Internet encounters memes. Memes are catch-phrases or images that resonate widely and call for imitation and repetition. They resonate. And because they resonate, they go viral.

In the eighth century BCE, two disparate prophets hinted at what today we would call a meme. It is an eschatological meme of peace, a hope for a world without war. Consider first Isaiah 2:4:

> He shall judge between the nations, and shall arbitrate for many peoples; they shall beat their swords into plowshares, and their spears into pruning hooks; nation shall not lift up sword against nation, neither shall they learn war any more.

And then, nearly identically, look at Micah 4:3:

> He shall judge between many peoples, and shall arbitrate between strong nations far away; they shall beat their swords into plowshares, and their spears into pruning hooks; nation shall not lift up sword against nation, neither shall they learn war any more . . .

It is no accident that these two prophets of Israel made a meme of peace. A longing for *shalom,* or wholeness and communal well-being, pervades the Old Testament. The psalmist rejoiced, "He [the LORD] makes wars cease to the end of the earth; he breaks

the bow, and shatters the spear; he burns the shields with fire"
(Psalm 46:10). The second-century rabbi Hillel said, "God could
find no better vessel of blessing for Israel than peace." Peace, he
said, was "the ultimate purpose of the Torah" (the first five books
of the Bible, central to Judaism). "Every single prayer of importance . . . ends with a prayer for peace and the hope that the same
peace that exists among the heavenly spheres shall also reign on
earth." *Jerusalem* means the cornerstone (*jeru*) of peace (*shalom*).

The peace meme is no less prevalent or important in the New
Testament. The word *peace* there occurs one hundred times, and
in every book except 1 John. Seven times the Apostle Paul refers
to the "God of peace," as in "The God of peace will shortly crush
Satan under your feet" (Romans 16:20; see also Romans 15:33; 1
Corinthians 14:33; 2 Corinthians 13:11; Philippians 4:9; 1 Thessalonians 5:23; and 2 Thessalonians 3:16). The Gospel of Luke (10:6)
refers to the one who embraces the gospel as a "child of peace."
Jesus's eschatological initiation of the kingdom bears peace as a
hallmark. Clearly, Christians were called to be a people of peace.
They worshiped the God of peace, and followed a Lord and savior
who was truly the "Prince of Peace" (Isaiah 9:6).

JESUS TEACHES PEACE

As we have seen, Jesus came announcing and inaugurating the
kingdom of God on earth. In so doing, he was bound to be asked
how followers could live in light of the kingdom. His most concentrated teaching on how to do that is found in the Sermon on the
Mount (Matthew 5–7). And in no small part his counsel is how to
live peaceably.

In this regard, two of his Beatitudes are especially worth con-
sideration. "Blessed are the meek," said Jesus, "for they will inherit
the earth" (Matthew 5:5). The word *meek* for us bears connotations
of timidity and obsequiousness. It is all about being passive and
downcast, being a doormat people can stomp on freely. But it is not
that in its biblical context. There, meekness encompasses a category
of positive and robust moral qualities: goodness, kindness, justice,

humility, mercifulness, and gentleness. It takes great strength and considerable character to live a good, kind, just, humble, merciful, and gentle life in a world so often given over to evil, cruelty, injustice, pride, pitilessness, and hardness. The one who does so is not passive, going with the flow, but vigorous, swimming against the stream. Likewise, Jesus says, "Blessed are the peacemakers, for they will be called children of God" (Matthew 5:9). Peacemakers live according to the nature of God, the very creator and king of the universe. What could be more genuinely powerful than that?

Later in his Sermon on the Mount, Jesus teaches, "You have heard that it was said, 'An eye for an eye and a tooth for a tooth.' But I say to you, Do not resist an evildoer. But if anyone strikes you on the right cheek, turn the other also; and if anyone wants to sue you and take your coat, give your cloak as well; and if anyone forces you to go one mile, go also the second mile" (Matthew 5:38–41). Again we may imagine a gross sort of passivity. And again we need to consider these sayings in their biblical and cultural context.

It is true that Jesus forbids resisting the evildoer like with like, violence with violence. You do not gouge out the other's eye if he has gouged yours. You do not knock out the other's tooth if he has knocked out yours. You will not descend into the spiral of violence or the cycle of revenge. What Jesus teaches instead is a sort of creative nonviolent resistance, a kind of moral jujitsu that turns the tables without injuring the other. To explain, I take the counsels one by one.

If anyone strikes you on the right cheek, turn the other also. Here Jesus imagines a context in which one with superior social status hits someone of lower standing. Such a superior would strike his "inferior" with the back of his hand, since only social equals would be struck with the open palm. So you have been struck on your right cheek as an inferior. But when you turn the other cheek, it is now impossible for the superior to strike you backhanded again. (Try it with a friend—but slap gently.) He can now only hit you with the open palm, which would be in effect to admit you are his equal. So the tables are turned.

If anyone wants to sue you and take your coat, give your cloak as well. Here we have to imagine a court of law where a suit has been brought to take someone's coat. Probably the defendant in this suit is someone who is in debt, and his only means of repayment are his clothes. Sued for your coat, you give it up. Now you stand clothed only in your cloak. Jesus says, hand over your cloak too. To remove the cloak is to expose your nakedness. Your consequent nakedness shames and embarrasses the plaintiff: you are naked as a result of his aggression. Once again the tables are turned.

If anyone forces you to go one mile, go also the second mile. In Roman-occupied Israel, it was not uncommon for soldiers to commandeer locals to carry a load for them. Galling as this was, the soldiers' superiors expected them to exercise restraint and not push the locals past the breaking point into resistance and even rebellion. So, Jesus says, if you have been enlisted by a soldier to carry a burden one mile, drag it two. Now the soldier must worry about his presiding officer's ire, that he pressed loadbearing beyond reasonable expectation. Yet again, then, the tables are turned.

In giving these three examples, Jesus is not covering all possible cases. He is inviting his followers to exercise acts of imagination about how to live peaceably and nonviolently, while not at the same time acquiescing to the aggressor's picture of how the world should operate (that is, unjustly and violently). At best, such creatively nonviolent acts of imagination may even change the aggressor for the better.

In any event, Jesus calls his followers to love their enemies and to pray for the good of those who persecute them (Matthew 5:43–48). And he teaches that we should be ready to forgive and persevering in forgiveness (Matthew 18:21–22). In all of this Jesus does not deny or duck conflict. In fact, he offers counsel on how to deal with conflict within the community of believers (Matthew 18:15–20). Thus, the peaceable and forgiving way of life Jesus commends is not one that turns a blind eye to injustice or expects to live in perpetual, supine placidity. Martin Luther King, Jr. spoke from deep biblical wellsprings when he said, "True peace is not the absence of tension; it is the presence of justice."

THE CROSS AND PEACE

Jesus not only taught the way of peace. He inaugurated the eschaton and lived it in his wonder-working actions, healing the sick, feeding the hungry, casting out demonic forces of chaos. In these works he brought *shalom*, restoring people and communities to well-being and wholeness. Supremely, however, Jesus lived the way of peace through the cross.

Israel in Jesus's time was an explosive and tumultuous place. The Israelites chafed under the yoke of the Romans. Many expected a messiah who would gather an army and expel the Romans. Others called for violent revolution even short of the messiah's coming. We may broadly call this movement for subversive violence the Zealot option. The Zealot option was a real possibility, even temptation, for Jesus. At his temptation in the wilderness, the devil teased Jesus with it (Luke 4:5–8). There Jesus rejected the option.

He rejected it again in Gethsemane, hours before his impending death. Jesus has prayed in agony and anxiety, to the point of sweating as if he was bleeding (Luke 22:44). He wishes the "cup" of the cross might be removed, but prays that if it is the Father's will, he will drink it (Luke 22:42). Then an arresting party of Jewish authorities and a "large crowd with swords and clubs" arrives (Matthew 26:47). Amid the tumult, an impetuous disciple draws his sword and chops off the ear of a slave of the high priest. "No more of this!" Jesus urgently commands (Luke 22:51). He heals the slave's ear, acting even now by the way of peace, of *shalom*. He says, "Do you think that I cannot appeal to my Father, and he will at once send me twelve legions of angels?" (Matthew 26:53). A Roman legion was comprised of 6,000 soldiers, so Jesus was saying he might easily have a massive army of 72,000 angels at this side. Instead, he chooses nonviolence, and submits to his arrest.

At his cross, as we saw in chapter 1, Jesus confronts and defeats the powers of sin and evil. By the cross, Jesus reconciles us to God, to one another, and to creation. Thus, as the Mennonite and ecumenical theologian John Howard Yoder puts it, "The cross is not a detour or a hurdle on the way to the kingdom, nor is it even the way to the kingdom; it is the kingdom come." The suffering "of the Messiah *is* the inauguration of the kingdom."

By his cross Jesus broke down the great dividing wall between Jews and Gentiles, "that he might create in himself one new humanity in place of the two, thus making peace . . . So he came and proclaimed peace to you who were far off and peace to those who were near; for through him both of us have access in one Spirit to the Father" (Ephesians 2:15–18). The event of the cross, a phenomenon of peacemaking, inaugurates the kingdom of God on earth. And henceforth, Christians will see the world in the light of the cross of peace. Even more, they will understand themselves as people who take up the peaceable, forgiving, servant-oriented way of the cross.

TAKING UP THE CROSS OF PEACE

Jesus Christ is the eschatological redeemer. Through him, God worked uniquely, and once for all, to rescue and reclaim all of creation. Christians, then, are not little saviors. First and last, they humbly point to the one true savior. So they dare not pretend they can be like Jesus lightly, or glibly. Yet it is the strong and recurring witness of the New Testament that they are to be like—to imitate— Jesus in one regard.

Franciscan monks once adopted the garb of the poor to be like Jesus. That was noble enough, but it is not how the New Testament calls us to imitate Jesus. Jesus was a carpenter and craftsman, but nowhere does the New Testament call us to follow him on this account. The Apostle Paul once wrote that he wished all might refrain from sexual relations, like him, but it did not occur to him to point to the celibacy of Jesus for our imitation. No, "Only at one point, only on one subject—but then consistently, universally—is Jesus [for the New Testament] our example: in his cross" (Yoder).

Consider, from a by no means exhaustive list, these representative texts:

Then Jesus told his disciples, "If any want to become my followers, let them deny themselves and take up their cross and follow me." (Matthew 16:24)

"Whoever does not carry the cross and follow me cannot be my disciple." (Luke 14:27)

[Paul and his companions are] always carrying in the body the death of Jesus, so that the life of Jesus may also be made visible in our bodies. (2 Corinthians 4:10)

[Look to one others' interests rather than your own, just as Christ] emptied himself [and took] the form of a slave [and humbled himself] to the point of death—even death on a cross. (Philippians 2:1–8)

For to this you have been called, because Christ also suffered for you, leaving you an example, so that you should follow in his steps. (1 Peter 2:21)

Therefore be imitators of God, as beloved children, and live in love, as Christ loved us and gave himself up for us . . . . (Ephesians 5:1–2)

[L]et us also lay aside every weight and the sin that clings so closely, and let us run with perseverance the race that is set before us, looking to Jesus the pioneer and perfecter of our faith, who for the sake of the joy that was set before him before him endured the cross, disregarding its shame, and has taken his seat at the right hand of the throne of God. (Hebrews 12:1–2)

We know love by this, that he laid down his life for us— and we ought to lay down our lives for one another. (1 John 3:16)

Thus, in this time between the times, Christians are called to bear the cross of peace. We are called to be peacemakers, nonviolently and noncoercively confronting conflict. We are called to forgiveness (Ephesians 4:32; Colossians 3:13), to love of enemies (Luke 6:32–36), to loving as Christ loved, giving himself up (John 13:34; 15:12), and to serving as he served (John 13:1–17; 2 Corinthians 8:7–9). All this is what it means to be Christians, people of the cross of peace, in the world and on behalf of the world.

ENGAGING THE PRINCIPALITIES AND POWERS

I have stressed that the peace Christians are summoned to exemplify is not milquetoast, bland, in denial of the reality of conflict, or merely passive. In fact, as the premier twentieth-century theologian Karl Barth had it, Christians are in "revolt" against the disorder and destruction consequent to sin. Far from placidly accepting the status quo, Christians in the light of eschatology see that Jesus and the cross of peace have confronted and overcome sin and forces of evil that often seem regnant in the world as it is. The world as it is is fallen, broken, and things are not as they should be.

In the light of Christ's victory through cross and resurrection, Christians are then called to resist the status quo of a lordless and disordered world. As the Canadian singer-songwriter Bruce Cockburn intones, "The trouble with normal is it always gets worse." What Christians resist is the normalized plight of humanity wrought by sin and evil. As Barth puts it, "The general plight against which Christians are commanded to revolt and fight is the disorder which both inwardly and outwardly controls and penetrates and poisons and disrupts all human relations and interconnections." Eschatologically, Christians cannot acquiesce to this disorder because for them it "is not a final reality that cannot be altered. Instead, it is a powerful phantom destined to disappear. Hence, even though they cannot do away with it, in all circumstances they must swim against its current."

The New Testament language used to pinpoint the nature of this conflict is that of the Principalities and Powers. "For our struggle is not against enemies of blood and flesh, but against the rulers [principalities, RSV], against the authorities, against the cosmic powers of this present darkness, against the spiritual forces of evil in the heavenly places" (Ephesians 6:12). The church does not battle to denigrate or in any way degrade actual, existing people ("blood and flesh"), but instead rebels on their behalf against "rulers," "authorities," and "the cosmic powers of this present darkness." These oppressive Powers pull on us, surround us, and threaten us at every turn. Yet the Apostle Paul is convinced "that neither death, nor life, nor angels, nor rulers, nor things present, nor things to come, nor powers, nor height, nor depth, nor anything else in all creation, will be able to separate us from the love of God in Christ Jesus our Lord" (Romans 8:38–39).

In fact, Christ, through his cross and vindicating resurrection, has defeated and disarmed the Powers. Subsequent to this work, with no less than cosmic ramifications, Christ reigns over the Powers.

> He disarmed the rulers and authorities and made a public example of them, triumphing over them. (Colossians 2:15)

> God put this power to work in Christ when he raised him from the dead and seated him at his right hand in the heavenly places, far above all rule and authority and power and dominion, and above every name that is named, not only in this age but also in the age to come. (Ephesians 1:20–21)

> [Jesus Christ] has gone into heaven and is at the right hand of God, with angels, authorities, and powers made subject to him. (1 Peter 3:22)

> For in him the whole fullness of the deity dwells bodily, and you have come to fullness in him, who is the head of every ruler and authority. (Colossians 2:9–10)

Now, today, and ever since Christ's work on the cross of peace, the Powers stand exposed and defeated. Yet in this time between the times they still rage, sometimes even more dangerously than before their defeat, just as a rattlesnake struck by a deathly blow presents the greatest peril. At the *parousia*, the Powers will be decisively and finally vanquished: "Then comes the end, when he [Christ] hands over the kingdom to God the Father, after he has destroyed every ruler and every authority and power" (1 Corinthians 15:24). In the meantime, the church witnesses to the Powers' defeat, to Christ's victory, "so that through the church the wisdom of God in its rich variety might now be made known to the rulers and authorities in the heavenly places" (Ephesians 3:10). As Yoder puts it, "The church does not attack the Powers; this Christ has done. The church concentrates upon not being seduced by them. By existing the church demonstrates that their rebellion has been vanquished."

But what, more precisely, are the Principalities and Powers? The Powers are social and cultural structures or practices that bring meaning and order to our lives. Directly in the world of the Bible, they include human traditions and customs, determined religious and ethical rules, mammon, the centrality of the clan or tribe, sex, and the state. These Powers still operate in our day. We may extend the list of Powers by adding contemporary phenomena such as class, race, national interest, public opinion, political correctness, the media, technology, fashion, the military-industrial complex, and accepted or bourgeois morality. The Powers also include ideologies or the various "-isms" that suffuse our thought, vocabulary, and social life: capitalism, socialism, communism, fascism, Republicanism, evangelicalism, secularism, postmodernism, terrorism, racism, sexism, and so forth.

Some of these Powers we could live well without (for example, terrorism, racism, and sexism). But we cannot live without any Powers, for they are the structures that bring order and meaning to our lives. In this regard, the Powers are good creations of God. The problem is that the Powers are also fallen. And in those circumstances they take on a life of their own. Humanity alienated from God finds its own creations overwhelming in their complexity and influence. The Powers are absolutized and demand unconditional loyalty. In consequence of fallen humanity's emancipation from God, the Powers operate in emancipation from humanity. As Yoder says, "These structures are not and never have been a mere sum total of the individuals composing them. The whole is more than the sum of its parts. And this 'more' is an invisible Power, even though we may not be used to speaking of it in personal or angelic terms."

So, as Barth puts it, the Powers "acquire the character of entities with some kind of existence and dominion of their own."

They win a certain "autonomy, independence, and even superiority" to people. Accordingly, "They are the hidden wirepullers in man's great and small enterprises, movements, achievements, and revolutions. They are not just the potencies but the real factors and agents of human progress, regress, and stagnation in politics, economics, scholarship, technology, and art . . ." Again, the Powers are in part good and necessary, but in their fallen autonomy they seek to be lordless and "make an impressive enough attempt to exhibit and present themselves as such." Thus the Powers are penultimates posing as ultimates. Absolutizing, they are susceptible and liable to idolatry, to total human investment and worship in practice if not in declaration.

To concretize this discussion of the Powers, I propose to sketch in more detail three contemporary powers: the state, the corporation, and the Internet.

The state gifts us with many goods. Law and government are salutary things, protecting us from a world of anarchy and brutish war of all against all. The state is responsible for the infrastructure, or roads and bridges and railways, that undergirds our conduct of business and the transportation necessary in our daily lives. Government provides and maintains parks where joys familial and national are celebrated. Government supports scientific research and artistic achievement. In a complex and error-prone world, government provides regulations that protect its citizenry's health and well-being. So much and all to the good.

Yet government exists in a fallen world, and is itself fallen. Particularly combined with nationalism, the state is prone to selfish interests, which at the worst lead to acquisitive and unnecessary wars. Empires, which are always a bad idea, see themselves as lords of the world—they colonize and subjugate peoples, and pretend to have no lords themselves. "The threat of change from might of right to the right of might couches at the door of every polity" (Barth). Fearful and desperate populations all too readily surrender political, social, ethical, and religious freedoms to a government vowed to protect them. We need only think of Germany in the pre-World War II era, beset by defeat, rampant inflation, and even hunger, entrusting power to Hitler and Nazism. Closer to home, the United States following the tremendous shock of 9/11 has succumbed to a disastrous war, to increasing surveillance, to reduction of rights, to drone warfare, and resort even to torture of actual or perceived enemies. Truly, the threat of the state as a Principality and Power can be dark indeed.

In such a situation, the church can only witness to the reality that the state does not reign supreme. There is a Lord beyond Caesar. The cross stands higher than any flag. Christians can only take care not to buy into nationalisms and their fevers. They will speak out against abuses of power, especially those wielded against or in neglect of minorities and those with the least power. They will work with those who call government to account and find their true security not in any worldly kingdom, but in the kingdom of God come and coming.

Next, consider the corporation. Corporations produce goods—from foods to lifesaving and life-enhancing drugs—that we all depend on. Corporations provide creature comforts—from air conditioning to a vast array of entertainments—that provide a standard of life (at least for the affluent) surpassing that of the most privileged royalty in days of old. Vast swathes of the population depend on corporations for their jobs and livelihood. Again, so much and all to the good.

Yet the corporation too exists in a fallen world, and is itself fallen. The modern corporation, by its own profession, exists for one means only: shareholder profit. Making a god of profit, the corporation ravenously subordinates all else to its pursuit. Employees are exploited and overworked. Regulations are resisted or ignored, and fatally faulty cars are built and sold, or pollution ensues, or workers are maimed on the job. In pursuit of profit, corporations expand and escape all accountability, so that we now have banks "too big to fail." Whether or not you believe in the existence of personal demonic beings, the corporation is treated under law as a person, and—particularly after the Supreme Court's 2010 ruling in *Citizens United v. Federal Election Commission*—arguably now possesses more rights than the individual citizen.

Once again, the church can only witness to the reality that Christ, not profit, is Lord and God. The church is a people gathered not for individual aggrandizement and profit, but for the good of the whole, attuned to the needs of the other. It exists to proclaim the gospel of the kingdom of the God of peace, and, especially when it meets shortfalls in the material needs of its members, embodies a different and more humane economy than the corporation.

Finally, consider the Internet. It is not difficult to rehearse the goods of the Internet. Most of us (among the affluent of the world) use it daily and with great gain at work and play. It enables us to communicate across the world, with friends or colleagues, in an instant. It provides access—again, instant—to vast stores of knowledge and information. For scholars and authors (like myself), it is a boon practically beyond imagination.

Yet the Internet also exists in a fallen world, and is itself fallen. The Internet has shaken and reshaped entire industries, especially the book and recording enterprises. Thus it has been a power of destruction as well as reconstruction.

Furthermore, in cyberspace I can exist apart from my actual embodied identity. I can pose as someone greater (handsomer, taller, sexier, smarter) than I am. Assuming a superior identity, migrating from my bodily existence, and accessing the Internet's near-omniscience, I can fall prey to the seductions of Gnosticism, or extra-bodily being and esoteric knowledge. These are actually false and impossible attributes, but they are intoxicating, and it is no wonder some become addicted to the Internet. When addiction occurs, it is always a sure sign of a Power at work, for addictions lord over the addicted, making a god of a substance or experience that should at best serve as a helpmeet or amusement.

Another sign that the Internet is a Principality and Power is its marked penchant for propaganda, catch-phrases, and slogans. Rather than sustained and respectful conversation or argument, the Internet often favors soundbites, or the 280-maximum characters of Twitter. Thereby rich and complicated truths are reduced and even falsified. Users, submitting to the limitations of the Internet, succumb to veritable shouting matches and verbal fisticuffs.

They are dehumanized and in turn dehumanize and demonize others in the process.

Once again, the church can only name a Power a Power. It can witness to the limitations and beware the dark sides of the Internet. It can in its communication refuse confinement to the reductions of the Internet, favoring face-to-face conversation (particularly in situations of conflict) over electronic flamethrowing.

So, in all their engagements with the Powers, Christians will be about naming and identifying them as limited and desacralized goods. Above all, shod in the footwear of peace (Ephesians 6:15), Christians will be on the side of individuals and communities over that of any Principality or Power. In taking the side of actual humans and not any earthly cause beyond them, Christians are the ultimate humanists. As Barth has it, Christians "confess solidarity at every point with man himself, they show themselves to be his companions and friends without worrying about his garb or mask, and they make his cause their own." They stand with the person in things big and small, "in hope venturing and taking with him little steps to relative improvements wherever he attempts them, even at the risk of often going astray and being disappointed with him" (and with themselves, we might add). In the end, this striving for peace on behalf of the human is an eschatological commitment. For "They must assist him in full commitment in this time between the times and thus bring him the promise and be with him credible witnesses that God, like themselves, has not abandoned him and will not do so, that his kingdom, the kingdom of the Father, Son, and Holy Spirit, has come and will come even for him, that Jesus Christ is his hope too."

Chapter 5

PRAYER

"**P**rayer maintains the equilibrium of the world." So said John Climacus, a monk on Mount Sinai in the sixth and seventh centuries. I love the breadth and daringness of Climacus's statement. But is it true? And if so, how can it be?

Wars clash and rumors of war clang. Tsunamis, earthquakes, and tornadoes devastate lands and populations. Economies, when they do not collapse altogether, teeter on the edge of implosion. Politics divide rather than unite. Families quarrel and suffer estrangement. Beside all this, amidst all this, what can the feeble prayers of the church or individual Christians mean? How can they be effective, let alone maintain the equilibrium of the world?

I honestly do not know what Climacus intended, for he did not elaborate. But I know what his claim means to me, and why I affirm it. Quite simply, because Christians pray, the world knows what it is to be the world. The church addresses God the Creator, and the world knows itself as a creature. It is not self-made or self-invented, or merely the result of random physical and chemical events in a sea of meaninglessness. Because the church prays in thanksgiving, the world knows itself as a dependent and properly grateful creature. Because the church prays for forgiveness, the world knows itself as a broken and needy creature. And because the church prays in the light of resurrection and new creation, the world can be a hopeful creature.

Put slightly differently, but more epigrammatically: Because the church prays to God as Creator, the world has a past, a story. Because the church prays to God as sustainer, the world has a present. And because the church prays to God as redeemer and restorer, the world has a future.

So only prayer can maintain the equilibrium of the world. Prayer rehearses, to God and before humanity, the narrative of God's creative and redeeming work. Prayer cooperates with the initiatives of a gracious God who hears the cries of his world. In prayer and by prayer we root ourselves in the eschatological narrative that alone can affirm, "All will be well, and all will be well, and all manner of thing will be well" (Julian of Norwich). And so is the equilibrium of an uncertain world maintained.

THE LORD'S PRAYER

But how, precisely, should we pray? Jesus, of course, was asked that very question. He responded with what we now call the Lord's Prayer.

> Our Father in heaven,
> hallowed be your name.
> Your kingdom come.
> Your will be done,
> on earth as it is in heaven.
> Give us this day our daily bread.
> And forgive us our debts,
> as we also have forgiven our debtors.
> And do not bring us into the time of trial,
> but rescue us from the evil one. (Matthew 6:9–13)

The Lord's Prayer is eschatological through and through. Consider it phrase by phrase.

Our Father in heaven . . . We pray to the Father, a privilege granted to us Gentiles only through Christ's kingdom come and coming. For before Christ's life and work on the cross, we were "strangers and aliens"; now we are "members of the household of God" (Ephesians 2:19). Furthermore, it is crucial to note that we pray in the plural, to *"our* Father." Sometimes we think we pray individually, then, secondarily, gather our prayers together on Sunday morning. We should think of it the other way around. We learn to pray in and as the church, then go to our homes and work with our individual prayers. As Karl Barth puts it:

> [Prayer] is not a matter of the private salvation and bliss of the individual Christian, for the individual Christian can call upon God as *our* Father. He can only do so as one among the brethren. Similarly, the brotherly fellowship of Christians, the Christian community, is not an organization for the common cultivation of the very private concerns of its individual members. Their invocation is as such a supremely social matter, publicly social, not to say political and even cosmic.

Furthermore, there is great comfort in the fact that prayer is fundamentally social. Sometimes, in the throes of depression, prayer drops off my lips with all the heavenward lift of a rock rolling off a log. A friend in the middle of a marriage breakup told me he could barely muster the strength or faith to pray. All he could do was mutter the Lord's Prayer before he went to bed alone. At such times, it is encouraging to know that since we pray to *our* Father, others pray for us and even in our place.

Lastly, in praying to our Father, we should not forget that our prayers are big as well as small. They certainly include personal and private concerns, but they are too small if they are confined to those. The "our Father" we pray to is the creator and redeemer of the universe. So, as part of the royal priesthood, we pray on behalf of all people (and all creation). We pray as the "provisional representatives and vicars" of the wide world (Barth). For eventually, when the name of Jesus Christ is revealed in all its completeness,

> every knee [will] bend,
> in heaven and on earth and under the earth,
> and every tongue [will] confess that Jesus Christ is Lord,
> to the glory of God the Father. (Philippians 2:10–11)

Prayer

Hallowed be your name. To hallow is to honor. So here we are praying "honored be your holy name, with all the grandness and tremendous significance that is due to it." Biblically, a name designates a person's character and reputation. It epitomizes how she expresses her deepest and truest self in outward relationship to others. In this sense, God's name is honored throughout creation, from atoms to galaxies. Sun and moon, all shining stars, sea monsters, hail, snow, frost, mountains, wild animals and cattle, and flying birds praise

> the name of the Lord,
> for his name alone is exalted;
> his glory above heaven and earth.
> (Psalm 148:13 and throughout)

Already all creation unstintingly praises God's name with and by its very being. Still, we await the day when all humanity will equally and fully honor God's name. The "decisive hallowing of the name" will occur with the "appearance of a new humanity" and "the coming of a new heaven and a new earth" (Barth). So long as the world is marred and disfigured by injustice and sin and death, God's name is not being honored as it should. We need and await justice and rectification. But on the last day "the LORD will become king over all the earth; on that day the LORD will be one and his name one" (Zechariah 14:9). Christians, zealous for the hallowing of God's name, pray that God may be honored, but even more that he will be honored comprehensively. This ultimate and only adequate honoring of God's name will occur by God's own expression outwardly of himself, in his final and apocalyptic intervention at the end of time. So here again Christians pray eschatologically.

Your kingdom come. Your will be done, on earth as it is in heaven. These are patently eschatological phrases and need little comment. Jesus directs us to pray that God's kingdom will come, that all of creation will be redeemed and restored. This is the "not yet" of eschatology. But Jesus adds the "already" of eschatology: we pray "your will be done—now—on earth, as it is done in heaven." In part, we pray so that we will learn to yearn. We learn to yearn

63

for the setting right of all wrongs, for rectification and justice. And we pray for everything—the small as well as the large—to follow God's will. So we pray for our health and that of our loved ones. We pray for good and humanizing work. We pray for our play, that it may renew us and connect us wholesomely to others. Compared to the universal restoration of the *eschaton*, these are "little" things, but they matter to us and to God. And how we act and habituate ourselves in the little things will determine big things, including the shape and growth of our character.

Give us this day our daily bread. This phrase is replete with biblical resonances. Perhaps what most stands out from Israel's history is the episode of manna in the desert (Exodus 16). Liberated from Egypt, the Israelites wander for forty years in the wilderness. Careful that the Israelites not go hungry, God sends down a flaky, gummy substance called manna, or bread from heaven. The manna appears with each morning's dew. The Israelites are instructed to collect enough for the day's meal. Not surprisingly, some in their insecurity collect more, but the surplus for the day "[breeds] worms and [becomes] foul" (v. 20). The lesson was clear: they were to trust God for their *daily* bread. Likewise, we are called to prevail in and ever renew our prayers, and trust God day to day.

There are also biblical and eschatological undertones to this phrase. Jesus prayed in light of passages such as Isaiah 25:6–8:

> On this [eschatological] mountain the LORD of hosts will
> make for all peoples
>> a feast of rich food, a feast of well-aged wines . . .
>> he will swallow up death forever.
> Then the Lord GOD will wipe away the tears from all faces, . . .

In such texts God promises a way of plenty, an end-time banquet or party in which none go hungry or thirsty, or have reason to weep. This party is a sign that God is acting at last to rescue his people from exile and abundantly see to their welfare. Jesus's feeding miracles were signs that the party should continue and would one day embrace the earth.

Prayer

In the meantime, we should not forget that we pray as a royal priesthood (1 Peter 2:9). Praying for daily bread, we are reminded now to pray for and on behalf of any who are literally hungry, and strive to see them fed. Asking for not more than our *daily* bread, we should share and not hoard our surplus. What is gathered beyond our needs, to the cost of those who hunger, breeds worms and stinks in God's nostrils (see Exodus 16:20). That the world could now be fed but so many are not, because of sinful politics and economics, is a reality that will suffer eschatological justice and rectification.

And forgive us our debts, as we also have forgiven our debtors. As we saw especially in chapter 4, God calls Christians to be a people ready to forgive. We forgive because God, through Christ's work, has first forgiven us. Forgiveness of sins is a sign of liberation from exile and the coming of the kingdom of God. Failure to forgive is a denial in action of this eschatological truth. I cannot say it better than N. T. Wright:

> As soon as someone in one of these Jesus-cells refused to forgive a fellow-member, he or she was saying, in effect, "I don't really believe the kingdom has arrived. I don't think Forgiveness of Sins has actually occurred." Failure to forgive one another . . . was cutting off the branch you were sitting on. The only reason for being kingdom-people, for being Jesus's people, was that forgiveness of sins was happening; so if you didn't live forgiveness, you were denying the very basis of your own new existence.

And do not bring us into the time of trial, but rescue us from the evil one. Jesus's inauguration of the kingdom included his confrontation of Satan, that power above all set on marring and destroying God's good creation. Jesus exorcised demons that possessed individuals and separated them from God, themselves, and their communities. Seeing how his disciples did demon-subjecting work in his name, Jesus said, "I watched Satan fall from heaven like a flash of lightning" (Luke 10:18). Here and on the cross, evil was confronted head-on and defeated. Because Jesus has vanquished the evil one, and was tried by him and overcame him in the wilderness

(Matthew 4:1–11; Luke 4:1–13), we can pray that we will not suffer a similar trial. In all events, we have been rescued from evil and its worst. This part of the Lord's Prayer calls us to resist evil in all its forms, whether seductive or horrifying, and assures us that we are not on our own.

All told, then, we see eschatology from the beginning to the end of the Lord's Prayer. To pray as Jesus taught us is to realize, as the New Testament scholar David Crump puts it, "Eschatology is the grammar of prayer. Prayer is the language of eschatology."

PRAYER AND PILGRIMAGE

We walk with faith in the time between the times. The end of our journey is sure. The *eschaton* will come, apocalyptically. Yet along the way there are many surprises and developments. God in his very omnipotence makes room for human decision and volition. God's ultimate goal for the restoration of all creation is sure, but his immediate intentions leave space for human cooperation and freedom.

There is ample biblical precedence for wrestling in prayer with God, and seeing his immediate intentions changed. Abraham wheedles with God to save at least a few people from a depraved Sodom and Gomorrah (Genesis 18:22–33). At the ford of Jabbok, Jacob grapples with an angel (or God himself?) for a blessing eventually received (Genesis 32:22–32). Moses frequently negotiates with God. Apparently Moses was a stutterer, and intimidated by public speaking. He wins God's approval of Aaron as Moses's spokesman (Exodus 4:10–17). At the episode of the golden calf, Moses debates God about the wisdom of wiping out the idolatrous Israelites. "And the LORD changed his mind about the disaster that he planned to bring on his people" (Exodus 32:14). God does not think it a good idea to institute a monarchy for Israel, but the people demand a king and God relents (1 Samuel 8).

In the New Testament, permission for us to wrestle with God occurs supremely in Jesus's example at the Garden of Gethsemane. In this intra-trinitarian debate, the Son struggles with the Father about a way other than the impending cross. Here the Son and the Father do not change their mind, but Jesus's intense grappling in prayer, to the point of sweating as if bleeding, suggests that the Father listens to prayer and is open to our considerations, agonizing or otherwise. And Jesus expects us to persevere in prayer, trusting that it will change things. In the parable of the Widow and the Unjust Judge, he is not afraid to suggest that we should argue with God just as the determined widow will not relent in her nagging of the corrupt judge (Luke 18:1–8). In addition, the Apostle Paul says that the Philippians' prayers will make a difference and "turn out for my deliverance" (Philippians 1:19). He expects that Philemon's prayers will soon reunite them in person (Philemon 22). Similarly, the author of the Letter to the Hebrews believes that prayers will reunite him with his friends "very soon" (Hebrews 13:18). The author of 1 John prays confidently for Gaius's health (1 John 2). And so on.

God deigns to make us "partners of Christ" (Hebrews 3:14). Barth can even speak of "codetermination of a divine action by a human action." He says,

> He is a God who in overflowing grace has chosen and is free to have authentic and not just apparent dealings, intercourse, and exchange with his children. . . . He for his own part will not work without them. He will work only in connection with their own work. Thus he is not so omnipotent or, rather, so impotent, that as they call upon him, liberated and commanded to do so by him, he will not and cannot hear them, letting a new action be occasioned by them, causing his own work and rule and control to correspond to their [prayer].

All this means we should take seriously (and joyously) our freedom in and with Christ. It is a real and substantial freedom. Our actions and our prayers—whether or not they are all answered, or answered as we would like—matter. We might compare our prayerful pilgrimage in the time between the times to a road trip. Our destination is set. But as we travel we meet surprises and difficulties. A road is under repair, and we must take a detour. So our route changes. We encounter delays with traffic jams. Perhaps our car breaks down and we must take another detour to find a mechanic or—as once happened to my neighbors—even replace the vehicle. We may go out of our way to stop at a famous restaurant or visit a scenic site. We may get lost and for a while wander in confusion, and yet again end up on a new route.

Similarly, as we journey eschatologically, we know our destination. The kingdom is come and coming. But what we do not know is our exact route. We may encounter switchbacks along the way. Or, more pleasantly, we may find a faster and smoother road than we originally anticipated. Our destination—the new creation—is up to God. Our route to arrive there is largely up to us. Along the way, biblically immersed prayer is our GPS, our map, our compass for successfully completing the trip.

ESCHATOLOGICAL THEODICY

As we journey and pray, there are unanswered prayers or, at the least prayers not answered as we would like. Illness besets and, despite prayer, lingers and may even become terminal. Or perhaps tragedy manifests, in the form of an incapacitating accident or a lost relationship. Violence may befall us and darken our lives. Perhaps we are in a turbulent and oppressive marriage, hanging on by our fingernails. Worse, we see or may experience a world shot through and tattered with injustice, resulting in desperate pain and even many deaths. Then our thoughts and feelings and prayer turn to theodicy, or the problem of evil and suffering.

In such circumstances, we struggle to make sense of a shattered world, whether personal or social. Of course, our struggles are not new. The Bible reflects wrestling with the questions of evil in its earliest books. From very early on, Christian thinkers tried to make some sense of evil and the disruption it entails. Sometimes theodicies bring a margin of comfort to praying sufferers. But basically theodical theories fail and fall short.

For instance, the book of Job has been read as a theodicy. Job suffers boils and other extreme personal discomfort. Most of all, he loses his entire family to death. However, Job remains faithful and in the end he is granted a new family. The shortcoming here will be painfully obvious to any parent who has lost a child. Children are not interchangeable. Even remaining or new children cannot erase the ache for the loss of a particular child or children. The face and touch of a given child is gone and cannot be replaced by the face and touch of another child. So Job as a theodicy in the end brings cold comfort.

For another example, one early Christian theodicy suggested this broken world is a vale of soulmaking. Tragedies spur the sufferer to grow in character or depth of soul. There is some truth here. Trials surmounted can make us stronger and more compassionate people. But sometimes trials are not surmounted. People are worn down and reduced to shells of themselves, and sometimes even resort to suicide. Again theodicy fails.

Theodicies especially quake and break in the face of injustices on a historical scale. The Holocaust. The Rawandan genocide of 1994. Early American genocide of the Native American people. The early twentieth-century lynching of blacks in the American South (tacitly approved in the North). Such atrocities should stick and stay stuck in the theological craw. Nothing can explain them away. No words, concepts, or theories are remotely adequate.

But if we should not strive for a theodical theory, we can in the light of eschatology reorient ourselves to the problem of evil. As we noted in chapter 1, the evil preoccupying the Israelites was that of exile. Biblically, the main theodical question was, will exile end? And if so, when? "How long, O LORD?" is the repeated refrain that rings in prayer down through the centuries.

> How long, O LORD? Will you be angry forever?
> (Psalm 79:4–6)

> O LORD God of hosts,
>   how long will you be angry with your people's prayers? . . .
> Restore us, O God of hosts;
>   let your face shine, that we may be saved. (Psalm 80:4–5)

How long, O LORD? Will you hide yourself forever? . . .
Lord, where is your steadfast love of old . . . ?
(Psalm 89:46a, 49a)

O LORD, how long shall I cry for help,
    and you will not listen?
Or cry to you "Violence!"
    and you will not save? (Habakkuk 1:1–3)

In Zechariah 1:11–13, even the angel asks and petitions, "O LORD of hosts, how long will you withhold mercy from Jerusalem and the cities of Judah, with which you have been angry these seventy years?" In the New Testament, the martyrs under the heavenly altar pick up the prayer refrain: those "who had been slaughtered for the word of God and for the testimony they had given; they cried out with a loud voice, 'Sovereign LORD, holy and true, how long will it be before you judge and avenge our blood on the inhabitants of the earth?" (Revelation 6:9–11). We may ring the refrain on into our own day and age:

How long, O LORD, will you allow African Americans to be treated as second-class and dispensable?

How long, O LORD, will innocents continue to hunger and die as war rages on in the Sudan?

How long, O LORD, must your own Holy Land continue to be rocked by oppression and terror?

How long, O LORD, must the rich get richer and the poor get poorer?

How long, O LORD, must abortion be resorted to readily, optionally, unnecessarily?

To this echoing, still yearning cry eschatology offers no concept or theory of theodicy. What it does affirm is that Christ has died for the sins of the world and has once for all struck a killing blow at the forces of evil. And eventually Christ will come again and usher in his kingdom in its fullness. Then all injustice will end, righteousness be restored, and all wrongs rectified. This is not a theodicy of concept and theory, but of action and event. It will be

God's action and event that alone can dry every tear and set every wrong to right.

It is the Christian privilege to be inducted into this eschatological narrative. Incorporated into this story, our pains will not be avoided or lessened, but they will be set in proportion and perspective. We will suffer our own toothaches and cancers, slights and injustices, but we will see them within the sweep of this great story about the kingdom come and coming. And there, none of our pains will stand as final or ultimate. For nothing can separate us from the love and power of God in Christ. Prayer in the eschatological register can be confident of miracles, of always being heard and answered—if not today, then in the last day.

Chapter 6

CREATION

As I have noted, the eschatological hope is not just for transformed humans, but for all of creation. Soil, plants, and animals—rocks and minerals, all flora and fauna—are expected to grace a new earth. The vision of the Old Testament prophets enfolds humans within a larger, teeming web of life, on which they are dependent and with which they thoughtfully and caringly interact. Consider these texts:

> The wolf shall live with the lamb,
>> the leopard shall lie down with the kid,
> the calf and the lion and the fatling together,
>> and a little child shall lead them.
> The cow and the bear shall graze,
>> their young shall lie down together;
> and the lion shall eat straw like the ox. (Isaiah 11:6–7)

> For I am about to create new heavens and a new earth . . . .
> (Isaiah 65–17)

> They shall come and sing aloud on the height of Zion,
>> and they shall be radiant over the goodness of the LORD,
> over the grain, the wine, and the oil,
>> and over the young of the flock and the herd;

their life shall become like a watered garden,
    and they shall never languish again. . . .

Thus says the LORD of hosts, the God of Israel: once more they shall use these words in the land of Judah and in its towns when I restore their fortunes:
    "The LORD bless you, O abode of righteousness,
    O holy hill!" . . .

The days are surely coming, says the LORD, when I will sow the house of Israel and the house of Judah with the seed of humans and the seed of animals.
(Jeremiah 31:12, 23, 27)

I will make for you a covenant on that day with wild animals, the birds of the air, and the creeping things on the ground ["fertile soil"—Ellen Davis translation]; and I will abolish the bow, the sword, and war from your land; and I will make you lie down in safety. (Hosea 2:18)

To step outside the prophetic canon, note this hope in Psalm 36:5–6:

Your steadfast love, O LORD, extends to the heavens
    your faithfulness to the clouds.
Your righteousness is like the mighty mountains,
    your judgments are like the great deep;
    you save humans *and animals* alike.

The hope and expectation of earthly re-creation and restoration does not abate in the New Testament. At Acts 3:21, the Apostle Peter preaches the "universal restoration" of the wide world. In Romans 8:19–23, the Apostle Paul has a groaning creation—the rocks and trees, the dogs and bees—eagerly anticipating the last day and its liberation from the futility of decay and disintegration. At 2 Peter 3:13, the author writes that, "in accordance with his promise, we wait for new heavens and a new earth, where righteousness [justice] is at home." Revelation 21:1 also looks ahead to new heavens and a new earth. In line with this expectation of a new earth, and the care thereby due the earth we now inhabit,

Revelation 11:18 darkly warns that God will destroy those who destroy the earth. More positively, John the seer gazes into a new creation populated not only by people, but all of creation:

> Then I heard every creature in heaven and on the earth and under the earth and in the sea, and all that is in them, singing
>
> "To the one seated on the throne and to the Lamb
>
> be blessing and honor and glory and might
>
> Forever and ever!" (Revelation 5:13)

John's cataloging of praising creatures apparently includes birds and angels (in the heavens), domestic and wild animals and "creeping things" (on the earth), worms and burrowing bugs (under the earth), and whales and octopuses (in the sea). It could not be more comprehensive.

The eschatological story, then, invites us to dwell on the goodness and everlasting significance of creation. Indeed, in Genesis 1, God does not wait on the creation of humanity to pronounce his creation good. Before Adam and Eve appear, the soil, plants, and animals are deemed satisfying and delightful in and of themselves. Pleasure and edification will follow from thinking on the goodness and the future of creation.

THE ORIGINAL ECOLOGISTS

The ancient Israelites were a people of the land. They occupied a steep, rocky, and semiarid country. Especially with droughts about every three years out of ten, there was little room for error—and no room for waste—in their farming and gardening. So it is not surprising that the Israelites were ecologically sensitive.

For the health of the soil, these farmers let the land lie fallow at regular intervals (Exodus 23:11). They took care not only for their own livestock, but for that of their neighbors: "You shall not see your neighbor's donkey fallen on the road and ignore it; you shall help to lift it up" (Deuteronomy 22:4). And: "You shall not muzzle an ox while it is treading out grain" (Deuteronomy 25:4). They recognized that the wildlife that sometimes provided sustenance should not be recklessly plundered: "If you come upon a bird's nest, in any tree or on the ground, with fledglings or eggs, with the mother sitting on the fledglings or eggs, you shall not take the mother with the young. Let the mother go, taking only the young for yourself, in order that it may go well with you and you may live long" (Deuteronomy 22:6). Notice how the mother being left free to breed again is explicitly connected with protecting the web of life—"in order that it may go well with you and you may live long."

Leviticus, for us, is one the most intricate and opaque of biblical books. The detailed laws, with their finicky concentration on purity and obscure dietary prohibitions, make little ready sense in our circumstances. Yet the overall drift of the Levitical regulations is clear. These regulations stipulate implicitly that animal life is protected except for a few edible creatures. As the biblical theologian Ellen Davis puts it, "[T]he dietary laws are 'the Bible's method of taming the killer instincts in humans.'"

So the ecological concern for plants and animals was not solely about human welfare. Remember, God declared flora and fauna good even before humans were created. Psalm 104 pictures God as the creator and provider for all creation, including the earth (vv. 5–9), "every wild animal," the birds (vv. 10–13), cattle (v. 14), trees (vv. 16–17), "creeping things" (vv. 20 and 25), wild goats, coneys, and lions (vv. 18–23). Psalm 148 shouts "Praise the LORD!" and then lists an array of astronomical bodies, weather events, land, and animals doing exactly that: sun, moon, stars, sea monsters, fire and hail, snow and frost, stormy wind, mountains and hills, wild animals and cattle. Simply by their being what they are, God's creatures worship and laud him. In the Bible, it is only humans who rebelliously resist and fail to praise the Creator. So here we have something to learn, humbly, from our creaturely neighbors.

God's care for non-human creatures, on their own account, comes through too in the story of the reluctant prophet Jonah. The prophet is content to let the evil city of Nineveh suffer God's wrath. He would rather not be bothered to proclaim salvation there. Finally, after spending three days in the belly of a giant fish, he drags himself to Nineveh and does his prophetic duties. Even then he is grousing and dissatisfied, complaining that he knew the Lord would have mercy on the nasty place. The short book closes with a rhetorical question directly from God to the prophet: "And should I not be concerned about Nineveh, that great city, in which there are more than one hundred and twenty thousand persons . . . *and also many animals?*"

All told, then, we may see the Israelites as the original ecologists. Ecology, simply put, is the tender recognition that we humans have our being in an intricate matrix of life, with the welfare of humanity, soil, and animals profoundly and delicately interconnected. For Israel, all creation is to be prized and respected. Israel's covenant with God includes the land and its creatures. Creation's welfare is Israel's welfare. Ellen Davis helpfully summarizes:

> Overall, from a biblical perspective, the sustained fertility and habitability of the earth, or more particularly of Israel, is the best index of the covenant relationship. When humanity, or the people Israel, is disobedient, thorns and briars abound [Genesis 3:17–19]; rain is withheld [Deuteronomy 11:11–17; 28: 24]; the land languishes and mourns [Isaiah 16:8; 33:9; Hosea 4:3]. Conversely, the most extravagant poetic images of loveliness—in the Prophets, the Psalms, and the Song of Songs—all show a land lush with growth, together with a people living in (or restored to) righteousness and full intimacy with God. "Truth . . . springs up from the earth" [Psalm 85:11].

JESUS THE AGRARIAN

Jesus was at one with his Jewish heritage in terms of ecological sensitivity. We know little about his youth. But, in addition to close study of the Hebrew Scriptures, he must have spent much time outdoors observing and adoring creation. I say this because writers and speakers draw from a repository of what they know best and most intensely, and Jesus's parables and sayings abound with natural imagery. References to the outdoor world of nature came, well, second nature to him.

Thus his parables draw again and again from the farmer's life, with allusions to seeds and growth on different quality soils, seedtime and harvest, and wheat infested with weeds. Jesus demonstrated the agrarian's appreciation of the human's place only within a larger, interdependent ecological whole. In addition, Jesus allayed human anxiety and insecurity by appeal to creatures in their natural state, sustained by God's providence. "Are not five sparrows sold for two pennies? Yet not one of them is forgotten in God's sight. . . . Do not be afraid; you are of more value than sparrows" (Luke 12:6–7). Sparrows were the cheapest of birds, sold for poor people's food. Even these God takes note of: if not how much more, then, is his regard for a person? Consider, too, Matthew 6:25–30:

> Therefore I tell you, do not worry about your life, what you will eat or what you will drink, or about your body, what you will wear. . . . Look at the birds of the air; they neither sow nor reap nor gather into barns, and yet your heavenly Father feeds them. Are you not of more value than they? . . . And why do you worry about clothing? Consider the lilies of the field, how they grow; they neither toil nor spin, yet I tell you, even Solomon in all his glory was not clothed like one of these. But if God so clothes the grass of the field, which is alive today and tomorrow is thrown into the oven, will he not much more clothe you—you of little faith?

Furthermore, Jesus was comfortable enough with the outdoors that he was not afraid to venture into the wilderness. Our forays into wilderness are confined to well-stocked camping trips and short hikes up a mountain. We must exercise some imagination to appreciate how the surrounding wilderness threatened ancient people—especially during the long, inky nighttime hours with no artificial illumination more broadly cast than the glow of a campfire. (In our more populated, suburban and urban, technologically advanced world, it is the other way around: our burgeoning presence threatens wildlife and the welfare of wild lands.) Wilderness was the space outside human control. It was the reality that encroached on the precarious fertility of cultivated land, was inhabited by creatures dangerous to humans, and was seen as the haunt of demons (see Isaiah 13:21–22; 34:13–15; Revelation 18:2). All of this makes vital background for the Gospel of Mark's one-sentence account of Jesus's sojourn into the desert, and his temptation there. This occurs early in Jesus's ministry, immediately after his baptism. Mark writes:

> He was in the wilderness forty days, tempted by Satan; and he was with wild beasts; and the angels waited on him. (1:13)

This sentence, essentially initiating Jesus's saving work, begs to be read in an eschatological light. It echoes Isaiah 11, with its classic prophecy of a Davidic Messiah and its picture of beasts of prey and tamer animals living in peaceable harmony. At Jesus's baptism (Mark 1:9–11), he is anointed with the Spirit and identified as God's Son, thus embedding him in the lineage of King David not only genealogically (Matthew 1:1) but spiritually and politically (see Psalm 2:7). Now he goes to confront Satan directly in his own territory.

Other gospels give fuller accounts of the temptation, while Mark is terse, simply noting that Jesus was tempted by Satan. Mark 1:13, in this English translation (NRSV), is broken up by two semicolons. The parts of the sentence, before the first semicolon and after the second, frame "and he was with wild beasts" with two other encounters. The first encounter is with Satan, Jesus's implacable foe. The second encounter is with the angels who "[wait] on him," serving as attendant friends. In between come the wild beasts, who are neither implacable foes nor close and easy friends.

Jesus does not terrorize or dominate the wild beasts. He does not make them into pets. He is merely "with" them. We know enough about the fauna of Jesus's time and place to make a fairly extensive list of the animals he may have encountered over his forty-day stay: bears, leopards, wolves, cobras, desert vipers, scorpions, hyenas, jackals, desert lynx, foxes, wild boars, wild asses, antelopes, gazelles, wild goats, porcupines, and hares. In Mark, the expression "to be with" frequently has the sense of a close, benign presence. So, as the biblical theologian Richard Bauckham puts it regarding the wild animals, "Jesus befriends them. He is peaceably with them."

In short, Jesus confronts Satan and makes peace with the wild animals (à la Isaiah 11) before he proclaims and enacts the kingdom of God among humans. It is as if he his establishing his messianic and eschatological bona fides before he enters the human arena as the Anointed One. His peaceful sojourn among the wild animals may be likened to his later healing ministry. He does not, with a mass gesture, heal every sick person in Israel. Inaugurating the kingdom of God, he heals some and so signally points to the later healing of all at the *eschaton*. Likewise, Jesus's presence among the wild beasts for forty days does not make the wilderness safe for any and all subsequent wanderers. Instead, it too is a sign of the inauguration of the kingdom yet awaiting its fullness, to arrive with the *eschaton*. How marvelous that Jesus's inaugurated kingdom encompasses not only human and demonic kingdoms, but the animal kingdom as well.

ESCHATOLOGY AND ECOLOGY NOW

What we said in chapter 2 of the human body can also be said of creation in general. In the Christian story, creation is triply sanctified. First, creation is made good and delightful. Second, Jesus's incarnation blesses all creation in addition to humans. Third, his victorious resurrection liberates all of creation. As the Eastern Orthodox theologian Paulos Mar Gregorios nicely puts it,

> Christ the Incarnate One assumed flesh—organic, human flesh; he was nurtured by air and water, vegetables and meat, like the rest of us. He took matter into himself, so matter is not alien to him now. His body is a *material* body—transformed, of course, but transformed *matter*. Thus he shares his being with the whole created order:

> animals and birds, snakes and worms, flowers and seeds.
> All parts of creation are now reconciled to Christ. And
> the created order is set free to share in the glorious free-
> dom of the children of God.

In this time between the times, then, Christians live with a deep and abiding respect for creation. Since creatures praise God simply by being themselves, we have much to learn by attentively watching and listening to them. Observe the playfulness of squirrels, chasing one another in spirals around the trunk of a tree. Heed the lion's majesty. Hear and learn the songs of birds, and regard their singing as praise of the God of life. (My favorite praise song may be the fizzy gulp-serenade of the starling.)

For too long in modern history, people have regarded nature on a mechanical model, as if it is no more than a brute machine, able to be taken apart and dissected with impunity. In recent decades scientists have become more ecologically aware, and approach creation as something intricate, animate, truly alive. Thus the nineteenth-century conservationist John Muir said, "[As breezes blew through,] I could distinctly hear the varying tones of individual trees—Spruce, and Fir, and Pine, and leafless Oak. Each was expressing itself in its own ways—singing its own song, and making its own particular gestures . . ."

Following in the footsteps of ecologically sensitive observers like Muir, contemporary foresters have discovered that trees possess a fascinating and inexplicable individuality. Trees of the same species planted in the same soil, climate, and spacing conditions actually grow at different rates, and with different levels of health. Individual trees seem to possess what we might almost call volition and selfhood.

Not all of us have the keen ecological sensitivity of John Muir, or the scientific training of foresters. But we can pay close attention to our pets. With no slight to cats and cat lovers, I am a dog lover. We have much to learn from dogs. Every day, they exult in life and being. Hospitable creatures, they love company. With their focus on scents and smelling, they draw our attention to the soil and the "morning news" that the dew-soaked grass brings. Living for

Creation

fourteen years with our smooth-coat collie, Merle, I learned much from his doggish qualities about how to be a better human being and Christian. Here, in the form of a poem, is something he taught me.

Lessons in Prayer, from a Dog

He assumes his still posture
two feet from the table.
He is not grabby,
his tongue is not hanging out,
he is quiet.

He wants to leap,
he wants to snap up
meat and blood.
You can tell.
But what he does is sit
as the gods
his masters and mistresses
fork steak and potatoes
into their mouths.

He is expectant
but not presumptuous.
He can wait.
He can live with disappointment.
He can abide frustration
and suffer suspense.

He watches
for signals,
he listens for calls
of his name from above.

At hints that
he may be gifted
with a morsel,
he intensifies his
already rapt concentration,
he looks his god in the eye,
but humbly,
sure of his innocence
in his need,

if his need only.

On the (often rare) occasions
when gifts are laid on his tongue,
he takes them whole,
then instantly resumes
the posture of attention,
beseeching, listening, alert,
the posture of hard-won faith
that will take no for an answer
yet ever and again hopefully
return to the questioning.

I cannot conclude this portion of this chapter without mentioning the premier ecological issue (maybe the most important issue, period) now facing humanity and all of creation. If Christians are to care for creation and all its creatures, we must take grave note of climate change. Our glaciers are melting, our oceans rising, our temperatures creeping upwards. Most climatologists believe human activities, releasing overbearing amounts of carbon dioxide into the atmosphere, are largely responsible for these events. We are resistant to this truth in no small part because the prevention or amelioration of global warming calls for us to radically alter our way of life. Driving and flying less, recycling trash, and turning off lights in vacant rooms are part of the answer. But larger economic and political changes are necessary to truly make a difference, to move us away from heavy reliance on fossil fuels. Because of our care for creation once made and to be eschatologically restored, I believe Christians should be at the forefront of those working for these changes.

I find the science of human responsibility for global warming frighteningly convincing. But I realize other Christians, particularly conservative evangelicals, argue against that science. To them I make the following appeal. True conservatives, as the term implies, are conservationists—conservationists of tradition, and of the earth they hand on to successive generations. They work for the future by caring about the past and its gifts. On climate change, the stakes are high, enormously high. If there is even the slightest chance the scientists are right, it seems to me conservative convictions and temperament necessitate caution and support for political and economic adjustments that will truly and most surely conserve an inhabitable environment.

In any event, the fact that God will transform the old earth is no argument for treating that old earth with contempt and reck- lessness. As we have seen, the biblical outlook expects care for cre- ation. (Remember, God will destroy those who destroy the earth [Revelation 11:18].) In no other eschatological regard do we let sin reign and ravage because we expect transformation and renewal. Persons die and await resurrection. Yet we do not counsel them to treat their present bodies contemptuously because those bodies will one day be resurrected. Exactly the opposite: we see this as grounds for careful and respectful treatment of our present bod- ies. So it should be with creation. In all our lives, including our ecological existence, we hope to build so that much will survive the purifying eschatological fire (1 Corinthians 3:10–15), to plant so that on the last day there will be more wheat and fewer tares (Matthew 13:30).

THE LUMBER OF LEBANON

It remains to discuss one other aspect of creation. Human culture, or the ability to enact it, is a gift of God. As sub-creators of the great Creator, we humans fabricate languages, make games, build cathedrals and skyscrapers, develop technologies of many kinds, write books and compose songs, and cultivate the earth and bear its bounty. Thus we prolifically elaborate and "fill the earth" (Gen- esis 1:28).

What will become of human culture in the *eschaton*? Once again we return to one of our main go-to prophets, Isaiah. At Isaiah 60, the prophet foresees a parade of nations into the New Jerusalem. The Holy City buzzes with commerce. Camels from Midian, Ephah, and Sheba come bearing gold and frankincense (v. 6). The flocks of Kedar and rams of Nebiaoth process in (v. 7). Ships from Tarshish sail to port laden with silver and gold (v. 9). Lebanon brings valuable lumber from cypress, plane, and pine trees (v. 13). "Nations shall come with your light, and kings to the brightness of your dawn" (v. 3). All of this will be enjoyed and put to work in Zion: "Foreigners shall build up your walls, and their kings shall minister to you . . ." (v. 10).

Again we see animals (camels, sheep, rams) in the new creation. But we also see products of human culture—from the activities of mining, gold and silver; from incense-makers, frankincense; from foresters, the lumber of Lebanon. Technologies are behind all these endeavors. Note, too, the "ships of Tarshish," which were known to be capacious and sturdy vessels, the work of expert shipbuilders. The kings represent all the excellencies of their various cultures, and they come in procession. (Revelation 21:26, surely influenced by Isaiah, also envisages the kings bearing the wealth of nations into the New Jerusalem.)

Shorn of their idolatrous tendencies, as Principalities and Powers now tamed and redirected to God's glory and human welfare, the works of culture will find the gates of the Holy City always open to them (Isaiah 60:11). We can expect in the new creation art and commerce, technology and service to God and one another, and surely much music. And of course, centrally, there will be another human innovation, the worship of God in all tongues (consider Acts 2:1–13).

Accordingly, it seems, work and play will have their places in the New Jerusalem. Play we can readily accept. But work may raise reservations. After all, work for us in the old creation is too often burdensome. Yet any of us fortunate enough to have good work here and now know of times when work in itself gives pleasure. We get into the groove and experience what the psychologists call "flow." The work comes easily and abundantly, a gift even as we exercise our gifts, and before we know it we have forgotten to stop for lunch. Such, I think, will be work for everyone in the new creation—an intrinsic good, enjoyed simply for itself and the praise of God it embodies and reflects. We will never get enough of it.

Taken as a whole, the eschatological story includes all the life and stuff of creation: skies and trees, all animals, and all of culture that is redeemable. So it holds out a picture of life everlasting much

Creation

more appealing than the bland and bored harp-strummers on clouds, depicted so often in such popular culture as the cartoons in *The New Yorker*. Said the biblical theologian G. B. Caird, "One of the reasons why [people] of our generation have turned against conventional Christianity is that they think it involves writing off the solid joys of this present life for some less substantial treasure [in an ethereal heaven]. . . . The whole point of the resurrection of the body is that life in the world to come is to be lived on a renewed earth. . . . Everything of real worth in the old heaven and earth, including the achievements of [humanity's] inventive, artistic, and intellectual prowess, will find a place in the eternal order."

Chapter 7

SEX

I asked a priest, "Will there be sex in heaven?" He replied with a wink, "I sure hope so, because I haven't gotten much on earth."

In fact, as the priest no doubt knew, the Christian tradition has mostly imagined there will be no sex in the new creation. Some church fathers even imagined there would be no sexuality or gender for our resurrected, transformed bodies. But this is clearly contradicted by Jesus's resurrected body, which was not androgynous but plainly male and masculine. So the tradition has usually envisioned a new creation populated by bodies of the male or female gender. Yet it has not taken the next step and affirmed genital sexual practice in the *eschaton*.

Still, I want to answer to the question of whether or not there will be sex with a yes, or at least a strong maybe. It is time, I think, to throw off the vestiges of Platonism that have retained a suspicion of the body and all its goodness (see chapter 2). That said, I do not take lightly the departure from tradition on this or any other question. A new reading of the Bible and the tradition always bears the burden of proof. It is clear, just the same, that biblical interpretation has changed—many times—over the centuries. Let me offer just two examples.

At Matthew 28:18–20 we find what has come to be called the Great Commission. "And Jesus came and said to them, 'All authority in heaven and on earth has been given to me. Go therefore and make disciples of all nations, baptizing them in the name of the Father and of the Son and of the Holy Spirit, and teaching them to obey everything that I have commanded you." We now read this as an exhortation to mission, that the church has an ongoing charge to evangelize and make disciples throughout the world. This reading is universally accepted and is not regarded as controversial. Yet the church did not always read Matthew's text this way.

In fact, it was not until the nineteenth century that our now common reading of Matthew 28:18–20 as the Great Commission became dominant. Earlier the church believed the command to "make disciples of all nations" had been fulfilled by the apostles, who went and did so in all parts of the known world. For centuries, interpreters focused on the baptismal clause, arguing it as a basis of the doctrine of the Trinity. As the evangelical theologian John Jefferson Davis counts, "Thomas Aquinas cites this text some nine times in the *Summa Theologica*. Two of these citations relate to the doctrine of the Trinity, five to baptism, two to other subjects, and none to missions." The great Reformers Martin Luther and John Calvin employed similar emphases in reading Matthew 28:18–20.

It was only in the nineteenth century, with an increasing awareness of the largeness of the world and the fact that the gospel had not been preached everywhere, that the Matthew text became known and focused on as the Great Commission. Changing circumstances, including the "settling" of Trinitarian and baptismal debates, resulted in an innovative reading of Matthew. Thus the Bible, capacious and ever fertile, remains always open to new readings occasioned by new circumstances.

For a second example of changing interpretation, consider the matter of slavery. The Bible contains no fewer than 326 references to slavery. All but two of them condone it, or assume it as a given part of the human social structure. It is only by reading the Bible by its wide narrative sweep, and focusing on the Golden Rule ("Do unto others as you would have them do unto you"), that we arrived at a reading of the Bible that condemns slavery. Now no serious commentator argues that Christians should accept slavery. But from the first through the nineteenth centuries, such was not the case. Once again changing social circumstances, occasioned in no small part by Christians who were struggling with the Bible, brought forth a historically new reading. Simply put, once it became clear that economic structures could exist without slavery, it made no sense for Christians to argue for retaining the practice.

Of course, neither of these examples prove that there will be sex in the new creation. But they do show how biblical interpretation, among faithful Christians, changes over time. They, and many other possible examples, give us permission to wrestle anew with biblical texts, and perhaps arrive at innovative and still faithful readings.

LIKE ANGELS IN HEAVEN

The most pertinent text that we have to wrestle with anew is Mark 12:18–25 (see also Matthew 22:23–30 and Luke 20:34–38). Here it is in full:

> Some Sadducees, who say there is no resurrection, came to [Jesus] and asked him a question, saying, "Teacher, Moses wrote for us that if a man's brother dies, leaving a wife but no child, the man shall marry the widow and raise up children for his brother. There were seven brothers; the first married and, when he died, left no children; and the second married the widow and died, leaving no children; and the third likewise; none of the seven left children. Last of all the woman herself died. In the resurrection whose wife will she be? For the seven had married her."
>
> Jesus said to them, "Is this not the reason you are wrong, that you know neither the scriptures nor the power of God? For when they rise from the dead, they neither marry nor are given in marriage, but are like the angels in heaven."

The Sadducees did not believe in the resurrection of the body. They refer to the ancient Israelite custom of levirate marriage, which was instituted as a kind of safety net to protect vulnerable widows. Implausibly, they imagine a succession of seven brothers dying and marrying the same widow. But however implausible—and no doubt argued to make Jesus's response harder—the question stands even if there were only two brothers dying. In the resurrection, who would be the woman's husband?

Jesus answers with some asperity. He tells the Sadducees they know neither the Scriptures nor the power of God. Then: "For when they rise from the dead, they neither marry nor are given in marriage, but are like the angels in heaven." Thus Jesus boldly and unrelentingly affirms the resurrection of the body. He affirms that, like the angels, the resurrected ones will be gifted with everlasting life. There then will be no need to procreate and extend the family name through time. So what Jesus affirms is that the resurrected ones will be like the angels in terms of immortality or invulnerability to death.

He does say there will be no marriage as we know it in the *eschaton*, but he does not say there will be no sex. After all, as we see in Genesis 6:1–4, the angels are capable of sex. So we need to carefully establish just what Jesus did and did not affirm. As the Catholic theologian Patricia Beattie Jung summarizes, "Jesus is not reported as saying specifically that there will be no sexual desire or sexual delight in this new creation. Nor is he reported as saying that already established marriages will not (in some transformed sense) be recognized." Of course, neither did Jesus explicitly confirm sexual desire and delight in the new creation. But he did not close the door on that possibility. What he explicitly affirmed is that resurrected ones will be like the angels in terms of everlasting life.

So a careful reading of Mark 12:18–25 does not rule out the possibility that there will be transformed sexual desire and delight in the new creation. At the same time, the Markan text does not affirm that such will be the case. We must look elsewhere to biblically affirm the goodness of sexual desire. And for that we turn to the Song of Solomon.

THE SONG OF SOLOMON

The Song of Solomon is easily the Bible's most sex-affirmative book. Admittedly, the church through most of its history has interpreted the Song spiritually, with Christ and his bride, the church, envisaged as the two lovers. There is validity in such a reading, but we must not forget the quality of metaphor. A metaphor only means with reference to the reality of the physical, concrete things or events it is based on. Take the imperative, "Get down off your high horse." Asked what that means, we say, "Don't be proud. You're really no better than the rest of us." But pressed on how it means that, we must picture an actual rider atop an actual horse, looming over the heads of the earthbound people around him. To come down off the high horse is to stand on level ground with the earthbound. So to say "get down off your high horse" is to say, "Get down from your lofty perch, get on our humble plane; after all, even Jesus only looks down on people from a cross." Just as this metaphor can only work with reference to physical people and physical horses, the Song of Solomon's spiritualized meanings can only make sense with resort to the very real and very physical reality of sexuality. We must allow the Song its plain as well as its spiritual meaning.

And the Song's plain meaning is lushly, overwhelmingly sensuous. It invokes and evokes the physical senses of taste, smell, touch, sight, and hearing. Wine, apples, raisins, nuts, honeycomb, and milk appeal to taste. Lilies, roses, myrrh, anointing oils, vines in blossom, and pomegranate and grape blooms appeal to smell. The lovers, in whole bodies and parts, appeal to touch and sight. The "voice of my beloved" sends the lover into rhapsody, appealing to the sense of sound (2:8).

The lovers are not afraid to give themselves up to intoxicating sexual desire and delight. "Eat, friends, drink, and be drunk with love" (5:1). She ecstatically adores her lover's face, head, eyes, cheeks, lips, arms, torso, and legs. He is even more exuberant in his delight in her body, hymning her cheeks (three times), neck (two times), eyes (four times), hair (three times), teeth (two times), lips (two times), breasts (three times), tongue, feet, thighs, navel, belly, nose, and head. One commentator, the Catholic theologian Paul Griffiths, even avers that 7:2 suggests the man's adoration of his lover's vulva. In any event, the vagina is poetically implied at 5:4:

> My beloved thrust his hand into the opening,
> and my inmost being yearned for him.

And the bodily fluids present in sexual play and intercourse are alluded to with a comparison to myrrh:

> I arose to open to my beloved,
> and my fingers dripped with myrrh,
> my fingers with liquid myrrh,
> upon the handles of the bolt. (5:5)

The lovers exult in sexual desire and consummation. Their bodies are playgrounds (he "lies" or lingers at her breasts and "wants to climb the palm tree to seize its fruit" [7:7–8]—Griffiths) and veritable gardens of delight. The body parts and sexual foreplay remind the lovers not only of abundant vegetation and its fruit, but of animal life, of fawns and gazelles at play and peace (4:5), and of mischievous foxes (2:15).

In short, it would be hard to imagine a more unqualified and exulting affirmation of sexual desire and delight than we find in the Song of Solomon. And while the Song does not denigrate procreation, its entire focus is on the joy and pleasure of sexual desire in and of itself. Finally, at 8:6, the Song drops an eschatological hint:

> Set me as a seal upon your heart,
> as a seal upon your arm;
> for love is strong as death,
> passion fierce as the grave.

Here the very sexual love of the lovers is imagined as a force capable of surviving death, a passion that cannot be denied even by the grave. Might this kind of love be transformed and present at the resurrection? Could there be sex in the new creation? It may be no more than an intimation here, but an intimation it is. And sometimes it is wise to take a hint.

A BETTER VIEW OF *EROS*

Whether we give a positive or negative answer to the possibility of sex and *eros,* or physical desire, in the new creation pivots on how we understand *eros.* Patricia Beattie Jung, following Grace Jantzen, argues that Plato conceived *eros* as born of need or lack. Then *eros* was only about filling a hole, an emptiness always wanting, and thereby prone to dependence and possessiveness. Thus bodily desires were naturally regarded as suspect.

But there is another, and more Christian, way of conceiving *eros.* God as Trinity is a perfect community, with the Father, Son, and Spirit in loving relationship one to another. In other words, God has never been lonely. God did not need creation for company, or indeed *need* it in any sense. God created out of the abundant, overflowing love of the Trinity. As we saw in chapter 1, God delighted creation into being, out of simple and passionate desire for more goodness and more beauty.

Accordingly, in God we have an exemplar of passionate desire that is not based in dependence or need. We can then see human *eros* as having "its origins in the extravagant overflow of abundance of the Creator's passion for beauty and goodness" (Jung). *Eros* is constructive. It springs from a pleasurable outpouring of creativity. So, says Jung, "We are drawn to what is beautiful and good, and our delight evokes or gives birth to a beauty and vitality within us. From this perspective sexual desire stems not from an inner emptiness or lack but rather from nascent attractions that mobilize us for relationship. As such, human desire is made in the image of our Creator's own passionate desire for and covenanting with all of creation."

Along these lines, as Jung notes, "Our hope is that passion will be quickened, rather than quelled, in risen life, so that we may love ever more generously and personally. There will be nothing greedy, controlling, or jealous about the relationships energized by the transformed desires we will experience in glory. They simply grow ever more tender, radiant, fruitful, and appreciative."

In other words, *eros* can be viewed as a positive good, an aspect of God's creation that reflects abundance, creational extravagance, and mutual love. *Eros* so conceived is, it seems to me, perfectly redeemable, right alongside and with our bodies, the earth, plants and animals, and our creative or work capacities. So viewed, it is not something best forgotten in the new creation. It is not part of the dross that will be burned away from the old creation, but of the gold to be purified and retained and honored there. Along these lines, note the Apostle Paul's reference to the genitals in 1 Corinthians 12:22–24:

> On the contrary, the members of the body that seem to be weaker *are indispensable,* and those members of the body that we think less honorable we clothe with greater honor, and our less respectable members are treated with greater respect; whereas our more respectable members do not need this.

Furthermore, I think we are at a point in church history when we are ready to make this move to a different, more ennobling view of *eros.* We may be suspicious of some of the results of the sexual revolution of the 1970s, but there can be no doubt today's Christians now view sex and the body more positively than our forebears. Ethicists across lines of Christian traditions now affirm sex not only for procreative purposes, but for its unitive goods. By *unitive,* they mean sex's capacities for binding lovers closer together, for promoting faithfulness to one another, and for enriching their relationship.

Thus, even among the Roman Catholic tradition, where birth control is most viewed with suspicion, the Church can endorse the unitive ends of sexual desire. As Vatican II affirmed in its "Pastoral Constitution on the Church in the Modern World":

> The actions within marriage by which the couple are united intimately and chastely are noble and worthy ones. Expressed in a manner which is truly human,

> these actions promote that mutual self-giving by which
> spouses enrich each other with a joyful and ready will.
> Sealed by mutual faithfulness and hallowed above all by
> Christ's sacrament, this love remains steadfastly true in
> body and mind, in bright days or dark.

Similarly, it is significant that among very conservative evangelicals there have been bestselling books such as *The Act of Marriage:
The Beauty of Sexual Love* and *Intended for Pleasure: Sex Technique
and Sexual Fulfillment in Christian Marriage.*

Perhaps, then, we are ready to imagine sex in the new creation. Like all else, it would be transformed and significantly different. We might take a lead from St. Augustine of Hippo, the great
African bishop of the fourth and fifth centuries. Augustine (who,
assuredly, had a darker view of *eros* than we are here portraying)
imagined that in the Garden of Eden, before the fall, Adam and Eve
had complete control of their sexual arousal. They could choose to
have sex when they wanted, and all their bodily parts would accordingly cooperate. Similarly, our passions in the new creation
would not be out of our control. We would will their activation and
the objects of their desire.

We would not be susceptible to sexual obsession (or idol-
ization). We would not be susceptible to unrequited love. And,
clearly, we would not be susceptible to sexual relationships in any
way abusive or harmful. Since there will be no progeny in the new
creation, there would need be no concern for an exclusivistic and
protective family unit for young children—a concern that it is vital
and necessary in this time between the times, where sex serves
a procreative purpose. Nor would sex receive undue attention or
emphasis. It would not overshadow the encompassing loves of God
and neighbor. It would not exceed our greatest joy and pleasure,
which will be the brilliant worship of God. It would leave plenty
of time for work, for (other) play, for enjoyment of new creational
animals and plants and vistas, and for feasting. It would be sex in
its place, but maybe—just maybe—in this place.

Sex

AGAINST PRESUMPTIVE ESCHATOLOGY

But if there may be a place for sex in the new creation, what does that mean for it, and for us, in the time between the times? It means we will treat sex with even greater respect and admiration. It means we will have a picture of *eros* that sees it in light of its ideal conditions: mutuality, reciprocity, deepening relationships. Just as eschatology, properly understood, increases our love and tender care for our present bodies and our present creation (the earth and all its creatures), so should it increase our love and care for sexuality.

But we cannot forget that we live between the times, and so still in light of the fall. Here and now, our sexual passions can too easily get out of control. Sex should increase fidelity, but in the conditions of a fallen world it can be the occasion of infidelity. Sex in a fallen world is a locus not only of betrayal, but of possessiveness and injustice. There are such things as incest and abusive and even lethal relationships. There are such things as sex trafficking and sex slavery. If there is anything to be learned from the television series *Law and Order: Special Victims Unit,* it is that the abuses of sexuality are endlessly and diabolically inventive.

Hence in the time between the times we are wise to take seriously the hedges or fences Moses and Jesus and the Apostle Paul built around sexuality. Here and now, sex is best reserved for marriage and committed relationships. If we pretend otherwise we fall into the trap of presumptive eschatology.

As we noted in the Introduction, presumptive eschatology irresponsibly grasps at the ending before the ending. It presumes upon the *eschaton.* It acts as if the kingdom has not only been inaugurated, but has come in its fullness. So, for instance, presumptive eschatology might assume there is no place for anger. After all, in the new creation there will be no call or place for anger. All will be well and all will be well and all manner of thing will be well. There will be no unfairness or injustice. But now, in the time between the times, there is still injustice, and plenty of it. There remains a place for righteous anger that compels us to protest injustice.

Likewise, there may be a place for *eros,* even if not marriage, in the new creation arrived in its completeness. But now, in the time between the times, sex remains volatile and frighteningly vulnerable to abuse. Thus there remains a place for exclusivity in sexual commitments and commissions. There is even a place for what might be called a righteous jealousy, though there will be no jealousy in the *eschaton.*

In summary, I have argued that the Bible gives us no definitive word on the possibility of *eros* in the new creation. I have argued that the Song of Solomon's full-throated affirmation of sex and sexuality cracks open a biblical door to affirming the goodness of *eros* here and in the kingdom come. Following Patricia Beattie Jung's pioneering work, I have argued that a reconceived and non-Platonic *eros* is imaginable for the consummated new creation. And finally I have reaffirmed a traditional Christian commitment to sexual exclusivity and fidelity in the time between the times. To say more than this is to venture into groundless speculation. And to say less is to fail to avail ourselves of gifts of the faith. Perhaps in the new creation the genitals will, like candles in the age of electricity, be sheer ornamentation. But I hope not.

Chapter 8

JUDGMENT

The world is in a hell of a mess. We might put it even more strongly: the world is in hell, a mess.

Always, the fallen world teeters on the brink of disaster. Throughout history, the world has careened from one catastrophe to another. Now we live under the threat of nuclear annihilation. Global warming destroys the earth, our island home. The US, powerful and rich as it is, faces a crumbling infrastructure and descent, for many, into conditions that used to be called "Third World." Clearly, we cannot save ourselves. Only the mercy of God sustains the world.

What entraps you? Perhaps painful illness lingers. Perhaps a friend or mate is estranged. Maybe a child strays into self-destruction. Maybe you suffer crippling debt. Maybe addiction burdens and defeats you. Maybe crushing depression bears down on you. What frustrates you, keeps you from flourishing, drives you to the brink of despair? Whatever it is, it is a consequence of living in a broken world, a world in the thrall of sin.

And even if your personal life goes swimmingly, do not forget that sin permeates our social structures. There is war and its devastations. There is inequity in economic systems, resulting in poverty and hunger. There is racism. There is sexism. We are, each and every one of us, under the shadow of the Principalities and

Powers. Sometimes we benefit, at least in the short term, from our position in oppressive social structures, from our class or race or citizenship in a superpower. We are implicated in injustice. We are trapped in sin.

In these dire circumstances, the church does not proclaim sin. Sin proclaims itself, all too patently and overwhelmingly. Instead, the church proclaims good news. God has acted in Israel and Jesus Christ to rescue his beloved (if faltering) creation. In Christ and his kingdom, the world has been liberated from sin. Christians have distorted the gospel when we have thought that we first must proclaim sin. No, we proclaim the good news of liberation, we proclaim that which (or rather, who) rescues us all from everything that entraps us. This is the great eschatological story: the kingdom is come and coming. It encompasses men and women and children and all of creation (maybe even, as we have just seen, sex). Today, Christ reigns. And eventually, wonderfully, his reign will be made manifest. Then sin and its power will be abolished. Every wrong will be put right.

THE NECESSITY OF JUDGMENT, BUT NOT ETERNAL CONSCIOUS TORMENT

If every wrong is to be put right, judgment is necessary. Sin must be vanquished. Reparations for evil deeds must be made. Those oppressed and hurt must be freed and healed. Bad habits must be relinquished and good habits put in their place. Life must replace death in all its forms.

And make no mistake: judgment entails pain. To take the comparatively trivial but thereby all the more telling example of bad habits, we know how difficult and even agonizing it can be to overcome them. They have brought us pleasure, of a sort. We have come to lean and depend upon them. Letting them go brings anxiety. We may even feel as if we cannot live without them. If this is so with bad habits, how much more so with radical changes in social systems, with costly reparations, with the demanding rectification required in ending oppression and healing its profound damage? But however painful judgment may be, it is necessary to set all wrongs right.

Thus, as Karl Barth said, "If [Jesus] were not the Judge, He would not be the Saviour." The eschatological story tells us that God has and will set all things right in Christ. Nothing that mars or disfigures God's good creation will last in the new creation. Bad habits, and much else, will be put aside.

Yet in recognizing that judgment entails pain, we must not forget that judgment is fundamentally positive. The biblical judge is not first of all one who sentences and punishes, but one who helps and saves. So in the Old Testament we see the judges coming to the aid of the wronged and helping the tribes and all of Israel when they suffer at the hands of neighbors or enemy nations. Judgment is about setting wrongs right. It is about saving humanity and creation from self-destruction and maladies at the hands of evil. The physician brings a painful but lifesaving sentence: "Quit smoking, or die young." Just so, God's judgment is at the service of God's salvation.

That said, we are ready to review the three options of the Christian tradition regarding the judgment of humanity and individual humans. I mean "options" in the sense that all three of these views date to the early centuries of the church. They each have orthodox proponents and have been adopted, to different degrees, by many within the Christian tradition.

The first option, dating to the second-century bishop Irenaeus, is called conditional immortality. The second option, dating to the second- and third-century Egyptian theologian Origen, and to the fourth-century Gregory of Nyssa, is universalism. The third option was codified latest, but actually came to be the dominant view of the Western church through most of its history. Its premier proponent was the fourth- and fifth-century Augustine of Hippo, and it is called eternal conscious torment.

By Augustine's lights, God predestined individuals to salvation or eternal damnation, which meant suffering forever the tortures of hell. Augustine was frank. Most people, even before they are born, are predestined to hell. A few will be saved. Those sent to hell will suffer endless retributive punishment. If this seems harsh, said Augustine, it is not for us to question. God proposes and God disposes. His will may be inscrutable, but only the foolish can question its justice, since God is God.

Of course Augustine strove to be biblical. He read texts such as, especially, Matthew 25:31–46, ending with the sentence, "And these will go away into eternal punishment, but the righteous into eternal life," and drew what he thought were the inevitable conclusions. Yet other estimable figures, such as Irenaeus and Gregory of Nyssa, read the Bible differently. We are, so to speak, within our rights if we do not take every cue from the great Augustine.

By my lights, the most serious objection to the eternal conscious torment view does not come down to any one biblical text explicitly on salvation or condemnation (though those are important), but to the central Christian story of the crucifixion. Eternal conscious torment contradicts what we know of God in his clearest and most profound revelation of himself—the cross. Jesus is killed by and on behalf of all of us. Remember, in the biblical schema the Jews and Gentiles were the two basic types of humanity (Ephesians 2:11–22). At Golgotha, some Jews played a hand. So, too, through the Roman Pontius Pilate and the soldiers who drove the nails into Jesus's wrists and feet, did the Gentiles. Thus we are all complicit in Christ's death.

We all, then, were enemies of God in Christ. Jesus not only died for his enemies, but asked God to forgive us with his dying breath (Luke 23:34). So the Apostle Paul wrote, "For if while we were enemies, we were reconciled to God through the death of his Son, much more surely, having been reconciled, will we be saved by his life" (Romans 5:10). Eternal conscious torment does not square with the nonviolent, enemy-forgiving, *agape*-loving God of the cross. The God of the cross does not seem to be the same God who would consign most of humanity to everlasting torture. And we must not try—indeed it would be blasphemous—to take back what God has given on the cross.

Relatedly, we must not fall into the error of opposing God's wrath to God's love. The Bible nowhere says "God *is* wrath." But it does say "God *is* love" (1 John 4:8). God is not schizophrenic, caught in a war between two contrasting impulses of wrath and love. His love envelops his wrath. It is the facet of God's love that will fiercely have nothing to do with the tainting or destruction of his good and beautiful creation.

As the pastor-theologian Fleming Rutledge observes, "God's judgment [is] an *aspect of* his mercy, not the opposite of it." She employs the brilliant image of a compass. The compass's needle points toward the North Pole and is repelled by the South Pole. "There are not two separate magnetic forces at work, but only one: the same magnetism that causes the working end of the needle to point north causes it to point *away from* south. Thus, to be '*for* us and for our salvation,' God must be against all that would threaten or destroy that purpose."

This, I submit, is the proper, cross-centered way to read the Bible on love and wrath, salvation and condemnation. Thus, with all due respect to Augustine, I set aside the prospect of eternal conscious torment. The God who would superintend an everlasting torture chamber, and that for most of humanity, is just not the God we encounter on the cross. Of lesser but still significant importance, this eschewal also does not offend against our human intuitions of justice. It does not demand that people suffer an infinite penalty—eternal torment—for the sin of a finite lifetime. This is like a litterer being sentenced to life in prison: the punishment is grossly out of proportion to the offense.

CONDITIONAL IMMORTALITY

The view of conditional immortality is built on a fundamental biblical truth. Humans were not created immortal. Only God has the property of immortal life in himself. In the Old Testament, people die and can no longer praise God. Consider Psalm 88:

> I am counted among those who go down to the Pit;
> I am like those who have no help,
> like those forsaken among the dead,

> like the slain that lie in the grave,
>> like those whom you remember no more,
>>> for they are cut off from your hand. (vv. 4–5)

> Do you work wonders for the dead?
>> Do the shades rise up to praise you?
> Is your steadfast love declared in the grave,
>> or your faithfulness in Abaddon [a place of destruction]?
>> (vv. 10–11)

Here the dead have at best a shadowy, lethargic existence as "shades," and are no longer capable of praising the God of life.

In the New Testament, eternal life is a grace of God in Christ. "For the wages of sin is death, but the free gift of God is eternal life in Jesus Christ" (Romans 6:23). Immortality, then, is not inherent to human nature, but a gift of God to believers (John 3:16; 1 Corinthians 15:50–54).

What then happens to those who choose not to accept this gift? Cut off from life, they simply cease to be. The Apostle Paul writes of their "eternal destruction" (2 Thessalonians 1:9). Jesus says, "Just as the weeds are collected and *burned up* with fire, so it will be at the end of the age" (Matthew 13:40). Second Peter 2:6 has it that the ungodly will suffer an "extinction" like that of the condemned cities of Sodom and Gomorah.

Where the Bible speaks of eternal fire, proponents of conditional immortality see the *flames,* and not that which they burn, to be everlasting. After all, fire consumes and reduces something to nothing. As the evangelical theologian John Stackhouse writes, "The final result of sin is death [Romans 6:23], as the fire of judgment purges the universe of the truly mortal remains of those who do not possess eternal life as the gift of God. Eventually, that is, all that cannot last forever turns to ash and disappears, no longer to pollute and offend and harm."

The conditional immortality view enjoys significant biblical backing. In addition, it has the advantage of not envisioning the unsaved as suffering eternal torture. "Finite beings can perform only a finite amount of sin, and therefore a finite amount of suffering is sufficient to atone for it" (Stackhouse). Finally, conditional immortality features an abiding respect for human freedom. As Irenaeus put it, "For God made man free. From the beginning he has had his own power, just as he has his own soul, to enable him, voluntarily and without coercion, to make God's mind his own. God does not use force, but good will is in Him always." The God of the cross will coerce no one into the kingdom. Those who choose not to accept the gift of eternal life will have their wishes respected. And eventually, as a consequence of their choice, they will fade into nothingness.

UNIVERSALISM

In our context, the first thing to notice about universalism is that it does not deny judgment. Universalists believe that in the end all will be saved, but only after suffering the judgment of God that purifies and redeems. The fires of divine judgment are (figuratively) real and seriously painful. Yet they ultimately are not retributive and punishing. They are remedial.

Universalism grounds itself in the cross. In the event of the cross, God acted to save his creation from the disfiguration and destruction of sin and evil. And grace upon grace, Jesus was supremely victorious on the cross. Nothing is greater than this event, where God's love rescued all of creation. As the universalist John A. T. Robinson put it, "Wrath and justice are but ways in which [God's] love must show itself to be love in the face of its denial." And finally, love prevails as salvation for all.

The universalists are not without appeal to specific biblical texts. Christ died for the sins of "the whole world" (1 John 2:2). "One died for all" (2 Corinthians 5:14). The Savior desires for "all people to be saved" (1 Timothy 2:4). Christ tasted death "for everyone" (Hebrews 2:9).

That said, there is above all a sweet eschatological symmetry to the long view of the universalist perspective. God created all. All are fallen and entrapped by sin. Christ died and was resurrected for all, and so all will be saved. The theologian George Hunsinger captures this with beautiful imagery in his contrast of the Augustinians (arguing for eternal conscious torment) and the Origenists (universalists).

> What is at stake, one might say, are two different views about how to interpret Scripture. The Augustinians hug close to the shoreline, so to speak, whereas the Origenists launch much farther out to sea. The Augustinians accuse the universalists of overlooking too much prominent timber when sighting the mainland, whereas the Origenists accuse the retributionists of not seeing the forest for the trees. The Augustinians would say that the forest is fraught with inscrutability; the Origenists, that any inscrutability is overridden by intelligible significance. The Augustinians would point to the rank undergrowth of sin in its great obduracy and abomination; the Origenists, to the towering peaks of divine love. The Augustinians would insist that faith must arise in this life as the necessary condition of deliverance; the Origenists would retort that the sufficient condition of deliverance is found in the assured persistence of divine grace.

Arguing for the "assured persistence of divine grace," the evangelical universalist Robin Parry writes, "Biblical justice is about putting right things wrong. As such, while retribution may possibly be a necessary condition of justice, it cannot be a sufficient condition, because retribution cannot undo the harms done and put right the wrongs. The primary end of God's justice, with respect to creation, is not punishment, but salvation."

Nor should we forget that a major body of the Christian tradition, Eastern Orthodoxy, has hewn and still hews to a hopeful universalist view. This view is winsomely encapsulated in a dialogue between one of the greatest Orthodox saints of recent times, St. Silouan of Athos, and another Athonite hermit.

> "God will punish all atheists. They will burn in everlasting fire."

> Obviously upset, [Silouan] said, "Tell me, supposing you went to paradise, and there looked down and saw somebody burning in hell-fire—would you feel happy?"
>
> "It can't be helped. It would be their own fault," said the hermit.
>
> [Silouan] answered with a sorrowful countenance: "Love could not bear that," he said. "We must pray for all."

Thus, even if we cannot be sure of universal salvation, we are not wrong to pray for it. Jesus desires it (1 Timothy 2:3–4). We are called to pray, to hope the best, for our enemies. Karl Barth writes, "If we are certainly forbidden to count on [universal salvation] as though we had a claim to it, . . . we are surely commanded the more definitely to hope and pray for it[,] . . . to hope and pray cautiously and yet distinctly that in spite of everything, . . . His compassion should not fail, and that in accordance with His mercy which is 'new every morning' He will 'not cast off for ever' [Lamentations 3:22, 31]."

SURRENDERING OUR JUDGMENT

Though I believe we should put aside eternal conscious torment (the love revealed in the cross truly cannot bear that), my mind is not settled on the matter between universalism and conditional immortality. Viewed far out to sea, the peaks of divine love tower majestically. But, hugging closer to shore, what about all the prominent timber of text upon biblical text that speak of destruction for those who do not avail themselves of the gift of eternal life? I know, the universalist might say the really prominent timber just is the wood of the cross. But still, what about all those other, specific texts?

In the time between the times, we do not have to decide. Put more strongly, in this time, with ambiguous evidence, we should not decide. We should especially not attempt to judge if specific people or peoples will not be saved. Jesus and the Apostle Paul are clear on this: God has taken away from us the right to pass any such judgment. "Do not judge," said Jesus, "so that you may not be judged" (Matthew 7:1). Says Paul, "Who is to condemn? It is Christ Jesus, who died, yes, who was raised, who is at the right hand of God, who indeed intercedes for us" (Romans 8:34). And: "For all of us must appear before the judgment seat of Christ, so that each may receive recompense for what has been done in the body, whether good or evil" (2 Corinthians 5:10). No one can rightfully judge another's servant (Romans 14:4). For Paul, we are not even to cast judgment on ourselves (1 Corinthians 4:3).

So we are not to arrogate judgment to ourselves. "It is our basic sin to take the place of the judge, to try to judge ourselves and others," said Barth. Only God, who alone can be trusted to be wholly just and merciful, can act as judge. In the face of sin and the destruction that threatens all creation and every individual, thus compromising God as Creator, God will judge. That judgment will begin with the household of God (1 Peter 4:17). So we must work out *our own* salvation with fear and trembling (Philippians 2:12). But we must not cast sentence on ourselves, and we certainly must not judge others. We know that whatever salvation comes, comes only in Christ and his cross. But we do not know what that salvation will mean for those of other faiths or no faith. And it is not our place to say.

So we are freed. We are freed from the dire if tempting burden of judging. We need not, we must not, cast sentence on others or even ourselves. We need not tiresomely struggle to prove our own innocence or convince others of their guilt. None of that is the gospel.

And we are freed to proclaim the work of Jesus Christ as first and last good news. We do not proclaim sin. We proclaim that which liberates people from whatever entraps and degrades them. Our focus, the focus of the gospel, is solidly, emphatically positive. The eschatological story promises great and grand things, things beyond imagining: the resurrection of the body, an immense dignity-granting of royal priesthood, the peace of the world, life-giving prayer, the renewal of all creation. The realization or at least a foretaste of all these promises is available now. Life everlasting, life abundantly, the Gospel of John has it, begins today, not tomorrow or in life after death. Thus God's gift to us, the gift we want to share with others, is not primarily salvation *from* hell, but salvation *to* the kingdom come and coming, and all the adventures and joys that promises. Help, invite, hope for people to run to that kingdom, not away from anything.

Chapter 9

THE ESCHATOLOGICAL

ATTITUDE

By now, it should be obvious that the eschatological story provides a way of seeing. Through it, we see the world and all that is. Seeing through the story of the world's end, we know how to view its beginning and middle. We see as people of priesthood, peace, and prayer. Our individual and personal projects are undertaken within the great project of God's creation and redemption of the cosmos. We are inducted into the grand mediation of a royal priesthood and the politics of a holy nation (1 Peter 2:9). We look at the world wherever it is broken and see Christ crucified, absorbing and bearing the sins of the world. We look at the world and see Christ resurrected, parabolically, wherever new life and hope spring.

All of our existence—all of existence, period—is comprehended by this great story and project of God. Nothing we can choose or that may befall us will stymie or exceed the limits of this story. So eschatology suggests and forms us with an attitude, a comportment or bearing, to life and death, to all that is and will be.

At its inception and throughout, the eschatological attitude is Jewish. The Bible is Jewish. For the Old Testament, this is obviously so. As for the New Testament, nearly all of its writers and main characters were Jewish. Our Savior was Jewish. It is by his Jewish life and blood that Gentiles are grafted into the vine of Israel's story (Romans 9—11), and made no longer homeless strangers adrift in the universe (Ephesians 2:11–22).

Thus, if our understanding of the kingdom come and coming is purely individualistic and does not embrace its social and political ramifications, our understanding is not Jewish enough. If our understanding of the new creation does not include all creatures, our understanding is not Jewish enough. And if our understanding of God and God's work does not include history and its unfolding, our understanding is not Jewish enough. "A Church that becomes anti-semitic or even only a-semitic suffers the loss of its faith by losing the object of it," said Karl Barth. I hope the chapters of this book have made it clear, then, how very Jewish—in the embrace of the social, of an eschatology including the material and the physical and all creation, of a God who deals in and with history—our Christian attitude must be.

What more can be said? By way of conclusion, I want to discuss how the eschatological attitude comports us so that we can bear tragedy, embrace irony, maintain calmness and equilibrium, and live with joyfulness.

TRAGEDY

The eschatological attitude gives us courage and the wherewithal to admit and face tragedy. We speak of tragedy when life or history visits us with brutal events difficult to assimilate. A death by accident or violence is tragic. A child committing suicide is tragic. A war, with its devastating effects, is tragic. We are rocked, shocked, knocked back on our heels by such events. Yet they are all too regular and real in a broken world. It will not do to try to deny or minimize the presence of tragedy in our lives.

In a deeper sense, tragedy occurs when no choice available will bring a happy end. Years ago, our family went on a canoeing trip down an Oklahoma river. My dad shared a canoe with my younger brother and sister. At a certain point we hit white water.

My mother and I, trailing Dad and my siblings in another canoe, lost control of our craft and crashed into trees at the banks of the river. Dad, thinking we needed help, ordered my brother to grab an overhanging branch and draw their canoe to a stop. One problem: the branch-grab did not halt their forward progress, but yanked my brother out of the canoe. Then the branch broke, leaving my brother flailing in the river. Dad faced a tragic choice. He could jump out of the canoe to rescue my ten-year-old brother, or remain in the canoe and keep my six-year-old sister safe. This story ended fortunately, even comically. At last my brother stood up, and the frothing water barely reached his waist.

But many times we are not saved from tragedy. For one thing, as finite beings with limited resources, we cannot help everyone who needs help. "For we live in a world wherein charity almost always must choose between lesser evils. The crucial question is how to sustain the life of charity in a world of suffering and tragedy, in a world where helping some means others cannot be helped," writes theologian Stanley Hauerwas.

For another thing, to live true to the faith means that we must sometimes make sacrifices that will bring harm to ourselves and others. This may mean living on a lesser salary than we might otherwise earn in order to serve the kingdom of God. In certain countries, it may mean suffering persecution both slight and dramatic, and seeing this inflicted on our children because of our faith commitment. At the ultimate degree, this may mean suffering martyrdom rather than relinquishing our profession of Christ died and resurrected as the true Lord and end of all life. As Hauerwas says, "To live morally . . . means that we must necessarily be willing to risk our own lives and others' lives for those values we find necessary to maintain our life together. In certain crucial cases, . . . we must be willing to let ourselves and others die rather than act against these goods."

The eschatological attitude does not deny tragedy and its role in our life. Instead, it provides a vision and way of life to live with, through, and beyond the inevitable tragedies that strike and pervade our existence. For Christ on the cross has taken human tragedy into the tragedy of his own torturous death. Our tragedy, like our sin, has been subsumed into the story of God and God's redeeming dealings with humankind. So, as Hauerwas puts it, "The church in its profoundest expression is the gathering of a people who are able to sustain one another through the inevitable tragedies of our lives. They are able to do so because they have been formed by a narrative, constantly reenacted through the sharing of a meal [the Eucharist or Lord's Supper], that claims nothing less than that God has taken the tragic character of our existence into his very life."

That is to say that God, in overcoming our sin and its disastrous effects, faced a tragic choice. He saw no way out of or through our sin except by taking on flesh and bearing our sin to the cross. There the Son of God suffered abandonment, even Godforsakenness, and so he knows firsthand the pain tragedy brings us: isolation, the agony of unhappy choices, acute physical and emotional pain. Henceforth, nothing we suffer can be foreign to the crucified God. We take courage to face and bear tragedy because we will never be apart from God in it. And we take courage because in the eschatological story, tragedy is not the last word.

IRONY

The eschatological attitude enables us to see and embrace irony. Irony deals in appearances that are not as they seem. Irony gazes beneath the surface to a deeper and surprising, even opposite meaning.

Screwball and his best friend, George, were pheasant hunting. As Screwball crawled through a barbed wire fence, his shotgun discharged and killed George. My Texas pastor friend was called to George's home. He found Screwball wailing inconsolably. He held Screwball in long hugs. He said everything he could think of that might ease Screwball's pain. He held Screwball's hand and prayed aloud. But still Screwball sobbed and keened. Just then, George's freshly made widow entered the room. With a tear-streaked face, she said, "It's all right, Screwball. If George had to be shot, he would have wanted you to shoot him."

Suddenly Screwball stopped crying, and from that moment commenced a long healing. Now, the statement from George's widow will not hold up to rigorous theological scrutiny. And surely it calmed Screwball because it was a statement of heartfelt solidarity from the only one closer to George than Screwball. But oddly, ironically, the words made sense to Screwball. They turned what he could before only regard as a terrible betrayal into an affirmation of friendship.

Irony is like that. It surprisingly turns things on their head. It opens up a new way of seeing things.

As the pastor-theologian Samuel Wells writes, "The tenor of an ironic story is one of contrast—between how things appear and how they are, between what participants are aware of and what happens in spite of them, between the *status quo* and its increasingly apparent absurdities. The contrasts of the Christian story are between human expectations and God's reality, between human failure and God's victory, between what one supposes to be the end of the story and the [actual] final end of the world."

In Christian eschatology, the ultimate irony is Christ's crucifixion. Here Christ's murderers mocked him with a crown of thorns and a sarcastic labeling of him as the "King of the Jews." Contrary to their demeaning intentions, they were actually dealing not just with the real king of the Jews, but with the king of the cosmos. The Principalities and Powers thought that, with the death-dealing cross, they were ridding themselves and the world of God's Messiah. Instead, God used the event of the cross to defeat the Powers and death itself. It is exactly, then, where God appears weakest that he is most powerful and effective, where God acts most humbly and stoops lowest that he acts with the greatest strength.

Thus, as Wells has it, an

> eschatological approach is intensely ironic. It sits in judgement over this time and this world; it mocks all who attempt to thwart its power—by arrogating power to themselves, by trying to evade death, or by behaving

as if impervious to judgement. All human efforts to con-
struct an earthly paradise are subsumed in a heaven beyond human imagining. All complacency is undermined
when the *eschaton* comes at a time no one expects. Apparent triumph turns to dust; apparent defeat is exalted.
The secrets of all hearts are revealed: neither the sheep
nor the goats know quite what to expect. The ethic could
best be summarized thus: it is better to fail in a cause
that will finally succeed than to succeed in a cause that
will finally fail. This is the language of profound irony:
beyond tragedy.

Eschatological irony means that Christians do not have to
give up even when all odds are stacked against them. Because "it
is better to fail in a cause that will finally succeed than to succeed
in a cause that will finally fail," Christians can be relentless and
unflagging in pursuit of justice and the protection of the marginalized. To restate what I said in an earlier chapter, but now from
a different angle, the eschatological attitude grants staying power
and resilience. If the Republicans are the last ones caring for the
unborn, the Christian will be among them. If the Greens are the
last fighting for a caring stewardship of creation, the Christian will
be among them. If the Democratic Socialists are the last ones fighting for the poor and the working class, the Christian will be among
them. If Black Lives Matter are the last ones believing that black
lives do matter, the Christian will be among them. If the relief
agencies are the last ones caring for refugees, the Christian will be
among them. If the pacifist anarchists are the last ones standing for
peaceable alternatives to war, the Christian will be among them.

So I note again what has been stressed throughout this book:
the eschatological attitude does not make the church or Christian
passive or uninvolved about the present. Christ's kingdom has
come. It is here today. And eventually it will be realized in its completeness. The ironic assurance that God's kingdom has come and
will come in its fullness gives us ground and confidence to act *now*
on behalf of justice and peace. It is hard, if not impossible, to keep
at a project that has no hope of success. But the carpenter who
is confident he can complete a house has energy and persistence

to build. The author who believes she can finish a book has the wherewithal to keep writing. Likewise, eschatology—with its assurance that God's kingdom has and will come on earth—grants strength to continue in the Christian life with zest and boldness, even to take on what others can only regard as lost causes.

CALMNESS AND EQUILIBRIUM

The eschatological attitude is one of possessed calmness and equilibrium. "Do not let your hearts be troubled," says Jesus. "Believe in God, believe also in me. . . . Peace I leave with you; my peace I give to you. I do not give to you as the world gives. Do not let your hearts be troubled and do not let them be afraid" (John 14:1, 27).

In the crucifixion of Jesus Christ, the worst that the world can do has been done. And with the world's worst, God wrought the world's best. God brings not only the world's survival, but its flourishing, out of the darkest of all human acts. In the time between the times, the Christian is possessed by a "peace that surpasses all understanding" because Christ has died and is risen (Philippians 4:7).

To be sure, this does not mean that the Christian escapes tragedy or suffering. But nothing that can befall us is now outside the compass of God's victory in Jesus Christ. The first and last thing the Christian has to say is: Jesus is victor. Thus a bedrock Christian attitude is one of peace, of calmness and equilibrium, even a certain serenity, in the face of the world's ongoing tragedies.

This is never an excuse for passivity. Rather, a bedrock equilibrium and even serenity gives Christians the wherewithal to continue to swim against the stream. Ever the enemies of injustice, Christians know that without the sustenance of the Holy Spirit, and the life-giving power of constant prayer, their efforts to fight injustice would soon leave them exhausted and embittered. But since we know the way the story is going to end, we stay with the struggle. We rest even as we are active, in the confidence that God never gives up on his creation. We are, as Barth says, in constant revolt against sin and the Powers. Yet our revolt and the energy for it is undergirded by the knowledge that not even the gates of hell will prevail against the church. Jesus is victor.

Eschatological equilibrium means that even if we temporarily lose our balance in the midst of earthly vicissitudes, we will soon and always regain it. We know what time it is. It the time between Christ's death and resurrection, and his *parousia*. We have a story that orients us no matter what happens, on a personal or a global scale. "Without a story," the Canadian cultural critic Naomi Klein writes, "we are, as many of us were after September 11, intensely vulnerable to those people who are ready to take advantage of the chaos to their own ends. As soon as we have a new narrative that offers perspective on the shocking events, we become reoriented and the world begins to make sense once again." I am saying that Christians have a narrative that orients and reorients us, that always helps the world make sense, whatever it may throw at us. Jesus is victor.

So our story is fundamentally, first and last, an affirming and positive story. Remember, we do not proclaim sin. Sin does an impressive enough job proclaiming itself. Instead we proclaim that the world was created good and has not been abandoned, but in fact has been rescued and redeemed, by its Creator, through Israel and in Jesus Christ. Accordingly, the eschatological attitude is not reactionary. True, too often Christians have been reactionary, resisting new developments in science and in social revolutions. Too often the church has been known by what it is against. But when this has been the case we have failed to grasp the depth of the eschatological attitude. Rather than resting on our fundamental equilibrium—the peace Christ brings to the world—we have succumbed to fear, to frustrated triumphalism, to an all-too-human but nevertheless unchristian anger.

I think part of this is due to a regnant but finally unbiblical eschatology that has understood the Christian life as a matter of drabness and sacrifices made in this life, so that when we die we might be rewarded with heaven and escape hell. Such a view leaves Christians simmering with anger. The world goes on having all the fun, here and now, while we give it all up for the hope of an escape to heaven when we die. But the eschatological story, rightly understood, is about induction today into the world tomorrow. It is an adventure we enter into, an enthralling journey we undertake, expecting, yes, that the best of it will only arrive with the *parousia*, but enjoying already the kingdom as it has come. And expecting, too, that the best and richest of this life will be taken up, transformed, into the new creation.

In the process, the eschatological story grants us the attitude of calmness and equilibrium. It makes it important that we attend to and tend our lives with gentleness and appreciation. We must not forget or let go of the everyday things that enrich our lives, under God's mercy. So, said the African-American theologian Howard Thurman, "The mass attack of disillusion and despair, distilled out of the collapse of hope, has so invaded our thoughts that what we know to be true and valid seems unreal and ephemeral . . . This is the great deception . . . Let us not be deceived. It is just as important as ever to attend to the little graces by which the dignity of our lives is maintained and sustained." The "little graces" Thurman speaks of are reflections of the Great Grace found in the life, death, and resurrection of Jesus Christ. And, like our membership in the royal priesthood, these little graces do maintain and sustain the dignity of our lives. Christians should embrace and affirm them in all their mundane forms, whether they occur inside or outside the church.

Stanley Hauerwas says something similar in a wonderful essay entitled "Taking Time for Peace." Hauerwas wrote the essay when the threat of nuclear destruction was at the forefront of the public mind. But even if we are now less keenly aware of it, nuclear destruction looms as a possibility. Even, or especially, in this shadow, says Hauerwas, one of the most important things we can do is embrace what Thurman would call the little graces.

> For it is my belief that there is no more powerful response to totalitarians than to take time to reclaim life from their power. By refusing to let them claim every aspect of our life as politically significant, we create the space and time that makes politics humane. Therefore,

there is nothing more important for us to do in the face of the threat of nuclear war than to go on living—that is, to take time to enjoy a walk with a friend, to read all of Trollope's novels, to maintain universities, to have and care for children, and most importantly, to worship God.

When Christians are known by what they are for rather than what they are against, they are living true to the eschatological attitude. This attitude grants equilibrium and calmness amid the shocks and setbacks of our lives. It gives us a sure place to stand, and even to fall. It is reflected in Luther's famous statement (even if he never actually said it), "If I knew the world was to end tomorrow, I would plant an apple tree today."

In God's good time between the times, take time to worship, to read a novel, to view a movie, to cook for friends, to walk the dog, to make love, to play with children. Take time to plant a tree.

JOY

The eschatological attitude is one of joy. For, as Karl Barth writes,

> Christ is risen; He is truly risen. Joy is now joy before the Lord and in Him. It is joy in His salvation, His grace, His law, His whole action. But it is now genuine, earthly, human joy: the joy of harvest, wedding, festival and victory; the joy not only in the inner but also the outer man; the joy in which one may and must drink wine as well as eat bread, sing and play as well as speak, dance as well as pray.

In the time between the times, joy is evanescent. It comes and it goes, fleetingly. But for Christians it is always an eschatological sign. It is a sign and reflection that in Christ God has acted, decisively, for humanity and his creation. Instances of joy point toward eschatological fullness and bliss. Thus even the dour and anti-Christian philosopher Friedrich Nietzsche could say, "All delight demands eternity." So joy is anticipatory. It foreshadows the *parousia*, the day when all will be put right and we will know nothing but joy, joy constant and everlasting.

I grew up on a farm. I know the joy of harvest. After a year of cultivating fields on a solitary tractor, harvest was the time when we gathered the combines and the trucks in the field, and brought in the crops together. There was playfulness in the work. On the combine, the wheat rows fell neatly before the sickles, the golden grain poured with gushing streams into the bin behind the driver. At the periodic emptying of the combine's bin, there were smiles and jokes exchanged between the combine driver and the truck driver. And at mealtimes, my grandmother and mother and aunt would bring feasts to the workers. Then we would rehearse the incidents of the day, exchange stories, and laugh often. I rarely enjoyed long hours alone on the tractor. But I loved the harvest.

The new creation will be a constant harvest. It will be an unceasing wedding banquet, an ongoing festival. It will be joy, joy shared and celebrated as a body. For joy is social. Good news demands to be celebrated. Who, upon receiving it, can not hardly wait to share it with friends and loved ones? We receive good news, and we are grateful. And our gratefulness overflows, reaches out to include others.

Joy is a recognition that life is a gift. Joy means accepting and embracing it as such. Really, joy is the simplest form of gratitude. "To be joyful," says Barth, "is to look out for opportunities for gratitude." Rather than being killjoys, Christians should be known for their keenness at being on the lookout for opportunities for gratitude and affirmation. Because "Christ has died, Christ is risen, Christ will come again." Barth is insistent and blunt. The one "who takes to heart the biblical message is not only permitted but plainly forbidden to be anything but merry and cheerful."

In the time between the times, life is a struggle. But it is punctuated by victories, by occasions for celebration. And it is undergirded by the promise that finally all will be well and all will be well and all manner of thing will be well. Through Israel and in Jesus Christ, God has acted to redeem and restore humanity, and the rocks and trees, the dogs and bees, as well. Against sin and death and all that mars or destroys creation, Life has spoken the last word. Through many years of struggle against South

African Apartheid, Bishop Desmond Tutu developed a distinctive and hearty laugh. "His laugh," says Fleming Rutledge, "is an eschatological sign of God's triumph over evil." Let such celebratory laughter have the last word, be the last sound. In the time between the times, we weep. But finally, conclusively, definitively, we laugh. Jesus is victor.

Appendix 1

READING THE BIBLE FOR THE FIRST TIME

I hope this book will be read by some who are relatively unfamiliar with the Christian story. And I hope it will urge all readers into the wonderful, strange new world of the Bible. For readers, new or old, however, the Bible is a daunting book (actually, a library). What follows are some suggestions for approaching and reading it.

1. Secure a translation in modern language. The King James Version is beautiful, but, having been done in the seventeenth century, contains archaisms that make it harder to understand. I suggest either the New Revised Standard Version or the New International Version. I prefer the NRSV for its gender-accurate language.

2. Read the Gospels. Go with the flow of the story. Pay attention to how the Gospels draw on the stories of Israel. Notice references to the kingdom of God (in Matthew, the kingdom of heaven) that Jesus comes to announce and inaugurate. Note how the Gospels climax in and devote special attention to Christ's passion, death, and resurrection.

3. Read and reread (it's short) the Letter to the Ephesians. Notice the worldwide and cosmic effects of Christ's cross and resurrection.

4. Read Genesis and Exodus. This will ground you in the basics of Israel's story and God-given mission.

5. Read Isaiah. This will introduce you to Israel's prophetic literature and give you a breathtaking glimpse of the Bible's eschatological vision.

6. Read the Psalms. The Psalms are Israel's prayer book. They refer often to Israel's history, such as the exodus from Egypt, and will soak you in Israel's frustrations and hopes, expressed through passionate prayer.

7. Now you're on your own. You may want to start at Genesis and read the Bible cover to cover. There are also lectionaries, as in the Episcopal *Book of Common Prayer*, that assign daily readings from both the Old and the New Testament. You will do well to procure a good study Bible, with notes that clarify the text. *The HarperCollins Study Bible* (New York: Harper-Collins, 1993) is excellent and grounded in state-of-the-art scholarship. *The NIV Study Bible* (Grand Rapids: Zondervan, 2011) is also solid and appeals to more conservative Christians. It's the more accessible of these two. You may also want to begin collecting and consulting commentaries. For a start, I commend "How to Choose a Biblical Commentary," at http://worship.calvin.edu/resources/resource-library/how -to-choose-a-bible-commentary/.

Appendix 2

READING KARL BARTH
FOR THE FIRST TIME

Few theologians are more eschatologically inclined and determined than Karl Barth. He makes for demanding reading: that needs to be said up front. But Barth is worth the effort. For adventurous readers who are interested, I make the following suggestions.

1. Read *Dogmatics in Outline* (New York: Harper and Row, 1959). It's short and provides an overview of Barth's thrilling biblical vision.

2. Read Timothy Gorringe's *Karl Barth Against Hegemony* (New York: Oxford University Press, 1999). It places Barth in his biographical and historical setting and provides an introduction to his key themes.

3. Read *The Christian Life* (London: T. and T. Clark, 1981). This book will nourish your spiritual life and give you a taste of the shape and substance of Barth's greatest work, *Church Dogmatics*.

4. With a head of Barthian steam built up, plunge into *Church Dogmatics*. A hint: Barth writes patiently and in detail, with lengthy biblical exegesis interspersed. It is not possible to read the *Dogmatics* in short snatches. Give yourself at least

an hour-long sitting with the text. Don't worry about comprehending all the details, but let yourself be caught up in the great oceanic prayer beneath and in the text—it will carry you along, and you will find Barth returning to and building on earlier exposition, so that his meaning will become clearer as you go.

REFERENCES
AND FURTHER READING

My theological lodestars are Augustine, Karl Barth, Stanley Hauerwas, N. T. Wright, and John Howard Yoder. It is unfortunately necessary here to issue something of a disclaimer about Yoder, since I use his words as an epigraph to this book and rely on his work particularly in chapter 4. Late in his life, it became known that John engaged in inappropriately sexual relationships with several (perhaps several score) female students. Especially because of the power differential, the relationships or incidents may even be termed abusive. There is no excusing this behavior. As to why I think we can still profit from Yoder's writings, even as we apply heavier scrutiny to what he says about power and relationships, I refer to two D's: King David and the Donatists. David committed shocking and grievous sins, yet we still read his Psalms and, if circumspectly, honor his name. The Donatists were ancient Christians who thought priests who succumbed under persecution could no longer be trusted or perform the sacraments efficaciously. Augustine successfully rebuffed this movement, arguing for the necessity of repentance but also for the faithfulness of God working through fallen people. John Howard Yoder had clay feet, yet what he said that was worthwhile remains, if only by the grace of God, worthwhile.

INTRODUCTION

On hunter-gatherer kcal consumption versus that of modern Westerners, see New Scientist, *The Origin of (almost) Everything* (London: John Murray, 2016), 68–69.

For those who care to read more about zombie stories and their resonance, a helpful resource is Kim Paffenroth and John W. Morehead, eds., *The Undead and Theology* (Eugene, OR: Pickwick, 2012).

Naming the Sense of Ending

For the end of the Sun and the universe, see David Wilkinson, *Christian Eschatology and the Physical Universe* (London: T. & T. Clark, 2010), 7–22; Weinberg quote, 21.

CHAPTER 1: THE STORY

Creation

I here lean on J. Richard Middleton, *The Liberating Image: The Imago Dei in Genesis 1* (Grand Rapids: Brazos, 2005).

The Election and Mission of Israel

The quote from Gordon Lafer is found in his essay, "Universalism and Particularism in Jewish Law," in David Theo Goldberg and Michael Krausz, eds., *Jewish Identity* (Philadelphia: Temple University Press, 1993), 196.

For an engrossing novelistic treatment of David's life, read Geraldine Brooks, *The Secret Chord* (New York: Penguin, 2015).

Jesus: Israel in Miniature

Throughout this and the following section, I am indebted to the work of N. T. Wright. For an eschatological overview at the popular level, see his *Surprised by Hope: Rethinking Heaven, the Resurrection, and the Mission of the Church* (New York: Harper-One, 2008). For Wright's account of the atoning cross, grounded in his inaugurated and holistic eschatology, see *The Day the Revolution Began: Reconsidering the Meaning of the Crucifixion* (New York: HarperOne, 2016). More intrepid readers will be repaid by plunging into Wright's scholarly works—here especially his multi-volume Christian Origins and the Question of God: *The New Testament and the People of God* (vol. 1; Minneapolis: Fortress, 1992); *Jesus and the Victory of God* (vol. 2; Minneapolis: Fortress, 1996); *The Resurrection of the Son of God* (vol. 3; Minneapolis: Fortress, 2003); and *Paul and the Faithfulness of God* (vol. 4; Minneapolis: Fortress, 2013). Wright's quotation, "Forgiveness of sins . . .," is from *Jesus and the Victory of God,* 268–69.

I am also indebted to the important work of J. Richard Middleton, *A New Heaven and a New Earth: Reclaiming Biblical Eschatology* (Grand Rapids: Baker Academic, 2014).

CHAPTER 2: HEAVEN

On Plato's dualism of body and soul, and denigration of the body, see Middleton, *A New Heaven and a New Earth,* 31–34, 283–96. For an argument that not all Platonic influences on Christianity should be rejected, see Matthew Levering, *Jesus and the Demise of Death: Resurrection, Afterlife, and the Fate of the Christian* (Waco, TX: Baylor University Press, 2012).

What About the Resurrection Body?

The quote by Anthony Thiselton comes from his *Life after Death: A New Approach to the Last Things* (Grand Rapids: Eerdmans, 2012), 113.

On Thomas Aquinas and the agility of the resurrection body, see Levering, *Jesus and the Demise of Death,* 119–20.

Joel Green is quoted from his *Body, Soul, and Human Life: The Nature of Humanity in the Bible* (Grand Rapids: Baker Academic, 2008), 168–69.

CHAPTER 3: PRIESTHOOD

A Royal Priesthood

The quote by J. Richard Middleton comes from his *The Liberating Image,* 90 (see also 231).

The quote by Alexander Schmemann comes from his *For the Life of the World: Sacraments and Orthodoxy* (Crestwood, NY: St Vladimir's Seminary Press, 1983), 61.

For the role of the priesthood in the Old Testament, see Walter Brueggemann, *Theology of the Old Testament: Testimony, Dispute, Advocacy* (Minneapolis: Fortress, 1997), 650–79. For an overview of the priesthood as understood in the Old Testament and the New Testament, see Richard D. Nelson, *Raising Up a Faithful Priest: Community and Priesthood in Biblical Theology* (Louisville: Westminster/John Knox, 1993).

The Temple and Eschatology

For this entire section, I am indebted to G. K. Beale and Mitchell Kim, *God Dwells Among Us: Expanding Eden to the Ends of the Earth* (Downers Grove, IL: InterVarsity, 2014).

For the centrality of the temple in Second Temple Judaism, see N. T. Wright, *The New Testament and the People of God,* 224–26.

Jesus and the Church as Temple

Here I continue to draw on Beale and Kim, *God Dwells Among Us;* quote, 97.

Living as a Royal People in the Time between the Times

The quote by C. S. Lewis comes from *The Weight of Glory and Other Addresses* (New York: Macmillan, 1965), 19.

CHAPTER 4: PEACE

Rabbi Hillel is cited in Willard M. Swartley, *Covenant of Peace: The Missing Peace in New Testament Theology* (Grand Rapids: Eerdmans, 2006), 33. The statistics on *peace* throughout the New Testament are also from this book, 5.

Jesus Teaches Peace

On meekness, see Swartley, *Covenant of Peace,* 87.

On acts of creative nonviolent resistance, see Walter Wink, *Violence and Nonviolence in South Africa: Jesus' Third Way* (Philadelphia: New Society, 1987), 12–34. For further prods to the peaceable imagination, see John H. Yoder, et al., *What Would You Do?* (Scottdale, PA: Herald, 1983).

The Martin Luther King, Jr. quote is in his *Stride Toward Freedom* (Boston: Beacon, 2010), 27.

For Christian pacifism as active (rather than passive) and confronting conflict, read Stanley Hauerwas, "Peacemaking: The Virtue of the Church," in *Christian Existence Today: Essays on Church, World and Living In Between* (Durham, NC: Labyrinth, 1988; rpr., Eugene, OR: Wipf and Stock, 2010), 89–97. This is Hauerwas at his most winsome and pastoral.

The Cross and Peace

The Yoder quotation on the cross and kingdom comes from John Howard Yoder, *The Politics of Jesus: Vicit Agnus Noster,* 2nd ed. (Grand Rapids: Eerdmans, 1994), 51. For popular-level introductions to Yoder's work, see his *The Original Revolution: Essays on Christian Pacifism* (Scottdale, PA: Herald, 1977) and *He Came Preaching Peace: Bible Lectures on Peacemaking* (Scottdale, PA: Herald, 2004).

Taking Up the Cross of Peace

For Yoder on the cross in the New Testament, see *The Politics of Jesus,* 95. Throughout this section I am indebted to Yoder's book.

Engaging the Principalities and Powers

On Karl Barth and revolt, see his *The Christian Life: Church Dogmatics IV/4: Lecture Fragments* (London: T. & T. Clark, 1981), 206.

Barth, ". . . is not a final reality," *The Christian Life,* 212.

Yoder, "The church does not attack the Powers . . .," *The Politics of Jesus,* 143.

Barth, the powers "acquire the character . . .," *The Christian Life,* 215.

Barth, they win a certain "autonomy, independence, and even superiority . . .," *The Christian Life,* 216.

Barth, "They are the hidden wirepullers . . .," *The Christian Life,* 216.

Barth, the powers seek to be lordless and "make an impressive enough attempt . . .," *The Christian Life,* 216.

Barth, "The threat of change . . .," *The Christian Life,* 221.

Barth, they "confess solidarity . . .," *The Christian Life,* 270.

Barth, they stand with the person in things big and small, "in hope venturing . . .," *The Christian Life,* 271.

Barth, for "They must assist him . . .," *The Christian Life,* 271.

References and Further Reading

For further reading on the Powers, I recommend starting with chapter 8 of Yoder's *The Politics of Jesus,* 134-61. Next, read Barth's treatment of the "lordless powers" in *The Christian Life,* 213-33. Hendrik Berkhof, *Christ and the Powers* (Scottdale, PA: Herald, 1977) is a short, clear, and pioneering treatment on the subject. Vernard Eller, *Christian Anarchy: Jesus' Primacy Over the Powers* (Grand Rapids: Eerdmans, 1987), is an accessible and witty overview. See also the treatment of the Powers throughout James Wm. McClendon, Jr., *Systematic Theology: Ethics* (Nashville: Abingdon, 1986). From there, adventurous readers will be rewarded by Walter Wink's Powers trilogy: *Naming the Powers: The Language of Power in the New Testament* (Minneapolis: Fortress, 1984); *Unmasking the Powers: The Invisible Forces that Determine Human Existence* (Minneapolis: Fortress, 1986); and *Engaging the Powers: Discernment and Resistance in a World of Domination* (Minneapolis: Fortress, 1992).

CHAPTER 5: PRAYER

John Climacus is quoted from ed. Thomas Spidlik, *Drinking from the Hidden Fountain: A Patristic Breviary* (Kalamazoo, MI: Cistercian, 1993), 355.

My thoughts on the church making the world the world are inspired by a often reiterated theme of Stanley Hauerwas's. For instance, he writes, "My claim, so offensive to some, [is] that the first task of the church is to make the world the world . . . The world simply cannot be narrated—the world cannot have a story—unless a people exist who make the world the world. That is an eschatological claim that presupposes we know there was a beginning only because we have seen the end." See Hauerwas, *Hannah's Child: A Theologian's Memoir* (Grand Rapids: Eerdmans, 2008), 158.

The Lord's Prayer

Barth, "[Prayer] is not a matter . . .," *The Christian Life,* 95.

Barth, ". . . provisional representatives and vicars," *The Christian Life,* 101.

Barth, the "decisive hallowing," *The Christian Life,* 116.

N. T. Wright is quoted from his *The Lord and His Prayer* (Grand Rapids: Eerdmans, 1996), 39.

David Crump is quoted from his *Knocking on Heaven's Door: A New Testament Theology of Petitionary Prayer* (Grand Rapids: Baker Academic, 2003), 299.

Prayer and Pilgrimage

Barth on codetermination, *The Christian Life,* 103. For more on this theme, see Crump, *Knocking on Heaven's Door,* 92 and 210.

Barth, "He is a God . . .," *The Christian Life,* 103.

I also recommend Donald G. Bloesch, *The Struggle of Prayer* (Colorado Springs: Helmers and Howard, 1988).

Eschatological Theodicy

Thoughts in this section were inspired by a reading of N. T. Wright, *Paul and the Faithfulness of God.*

CHAPTER 6: CREATION

The Original Ecologists

The quote by Ellen F. Davis, "[T]he dietary laws . . .," comes from her *Scripture, Culture, and Agriculture: An Agrarian Reading of the Bible* (New York: Cambridge University Press, 2009), 95 (internal quote from Jacob Milgrom).

Davis, "Overall, from a biblical perspective . . .," *Scripture, Culture, and Agriculture,* 8.

Jesus the Agrarian

This section owes much to Richard Bauckham, *Living with Other Creatures: Green Exegesis and Theology* (Waco, TX: Baylor University Press, 2011), esp. 111–32.

Bauckham quote, *Living with Other Creatures*, 76.

The Gregorios quote is from ed. Andrew Linzey and Tom Regan, *Animals and Chrisitianity: A Book of Readings* (Eugene, OR: Wipf and Stock, 1990), 27.

Eschatology and Ecology Now

For the John Muir quote, and concerning the individuality and volition of trees, see Brian J. Walsh, Marianne B. Karsh, and Nik Ansell, "Trees, Forestry, and the Responsiveness of Creation," *Cross Currents* http://www.crosscurrents.org/trees.htm.

"Lessons in Prayer, from a Dog" originally appeared in *The Christian Century,* February 12, 2008. I am grateful to the magazine's editors for permission to reproduce it here.

If you read one book on climate change, let it be Naomi Klein, *This Changes Everything: Capitalism vs the Climate* (New York: Simon and Schuster, 2014).

The Lumber of Lebanon

This section is undergirded by Richard J. Mouw, *When the Kings Come Marching In: Isaiah and the New Jerusalem* (Grand Rapids: Eerdmans, 1983). See also the essay by John Jefferson Davis, "Will There Be *New* Work in the New Creation?," in his *Practicing Ministry in the Presence of God: Theological Reflections on Ministry and the Christian Life* (Eugene, OR: Cascade: 2015), 271–89.

G. B. Caird is quoted from Levering, *Jesus and the Demise of Death,* 137, note 42.

CHAPTER 7: SEX

On the interpretation of Matthew 28:18–20, see John Jefferson Davis, "'Teaching Them to Observe All that I Have Commanded You': The History of the Interpretation of the 'Great Commission' and Implications for Marketplace Ministries," in his *Practicing Ministry in the Presence of God,* 158–75, quotation 162.

On slavery and 326 biblical texts, see Wesley Granberg-Michaelson's foreword to James V. Brownson, *Bible, Gender, Sexuality: Reframing the Church's Debate on Same-Sex Relationships* (Grand Rapids: Eerdmans, 2013), x.

On the history of biblical interpretation on slavery, see Willard M. Swartley, *Slavery, Sabbath, War, and Women: Case Issues in Biblical Interpretation* (Scottdale, PA: Herald, 1983), 31–64. Regarding pre-Civil War readings of the Bible in the American South, see Elizabeth Fox-Genovese and Eugene D. Genovese, *The Mind of the Master Class: History and Faith in the Southern Slaveholders' Worldview* (Cambridge: Cambridge University Press, 2005).

Like Angels in Heaven

For the reading of Mark 12:18–25 as focused on immortality (or, better, everlasting life), see N. T. Wright, *The Resurrection of the Son of God,* 422–23.

On the angels as capable of sex in Genesis 6, see Gregory A. Boyd, *The Crucifixion of the Warrior God: Interpreting the Old Testament's Violent Portraits of God in Light of the Cross,* 2 vols. (Minneapolis: Fortress, 2017), 2:1127, 1139.

Patricia Beattie Jung, "Jesus is not reported . . .," see her *Sex on Earth as in Heaven: A Christian Eschatology of Desire* (Albany, NY: State University of New York Press, 2017), 66.

For Paul Griffiths, see his *Song of Songs: Brazos Theological Commentary on the Bible* (Grand Rapids: Brazos, 2011), 149, 69.

A Better View of *Eros*

For Jung on *eros*, see *Sex on Earth as in Heaven*, 75–85.

Jung, *eros* as having "its origins in . . .," *Sex on Earth as in Heaven*, 80.

Jung, "We are drawn . . .," *Sex on Earth as in Heaven*, 109–10.

Jung, "Our hope is that . . .," *Sex on Earth as in Heaven*, 107.

For the quote from Vatican II, see ed. Austin P. Flannery, "Pastoral Constitution on the Church in the Modern World," 49, in *Documents of Vatican II*, new rev. ed. (Grand Rapids: Eerdmans, 1984), 952.

For Augustine on controlled sexual passion, see *City of God*, book 14, chapter 23.

CHAPTER 8: JUDGMENT

The Necessity of Judgment, but Not Eternal Conscious Torment

Barth, "If [Jesus] were not the judge . . .," see Barth, *Church Dogmatics* IV/1.1 (Edinburgh: T. & T. Clark, 1956), 217.

For a helpful orientation on the three orthodox views on salvation and damnation, see David J. Powys, *'Hell': A Hard Look at a Hard Question* (Eugene, OR: Wipf and Stock, 1997), 2–16.

For an incisive overview of Augustine on eternal conscious torment, see George Hunsinger, *Disruptive Grace: Studies in the Theology of Karl Barth* (Grand Rapids: Eerdmans, 2000), 229–34.

Fleming Rutledge is quoted from her *The Crucifixion: Understanding the Death of Jesus Christ* (Grand Rapids: Eerdmans, 2015), 317.

Conditional Immortality

For a succinct and able presentation of the conditional immortality view, see John G. Stackhouse, Jr., "Terminal Punishment," in

References and Further Reading

Preston Sprinkle, ed., *Four Views on Hell*, 2nd ed. (Grand Rapids: Zondervan, 2016), 61–81.

Stackhouse, "The final result of sin . . .," "Terminal Punishment," 64.

Stackhouse, "Finite beings can perform . . .," "Terminal Punishment," 79.

Irenaeus is quoted from his *The Scandal of the Incarnation* (originally *Against the Heresies*), (San Francisco: Ignatius, 1990), book 4, chapter 37.

Universalism

An excellent brief presentation of universalism is Robin A. Parry, "A Universalist View," in *Four Views on Hell*, 101–27.

Hunsinger, "What is at stake . . .," *Disruptive Grace*, 239.

Parry, "Biblical justice is about . . .," "A Universalist View," 113.

For an overview of Eastern Orthodoxy on universalism, see Andrew Louth, "Eastern Orthodox Eschatology," in Jerry L. Walls, ed., *The Oxford Handbook of Eschatology* (New York: Oxford University Press, 2008), 233–47. For the conversation between St. Silouan and the other hermit, 246.

Barth, "If we are certainly forbidden . . .," *Church Dogmatics* IV/3 (Edinburgh: T. & T. Clark, 1961), 478.

Surrendering Our Judgment

Barth, "It is our basic sin . . .," *Church Dogmatics* IV/1.1, 235.

On salvation "to" rather than salvation "from," I am indebted to Powys, *'Hell': A Hard Look at a Hard Question*, 418.

CHAPTER 9: THE ESCHATOLOGICAL ATTITUDE

Barth, "A church that . . .," *Church Dogmatics* II/2 (Edinburgh: T. & T. Clark, 1958), 234.

Tragedy

Hauerwas, "For we live . . .," Stanley Hauerwas, *Truthfulness and Tragedy: Further Investigations in Christian Ethics* (Notre Dame, IN: University of Notre Dame Press, 1977), 138.

Hauerwas, "To live morally . . .," *Truthfulness and Tragedy,* 69.

Hauerwas, "The church in its profoundest expression . . .," Stanley Hauerwas, *A Community of Character: Toward a Constructive Christian Social Ethic* (Notre Dame, IN: University of Notre Dame Press, 1981), 108.

Irony

Wells, "The tenor of an ironic story . . .," Samuel Wells, *Transforming Fate into Destiny: The Theological Ethics of Stanley Hauerwas* (Carlisle, UK: Paternoster, 1998), 166–67.

Wells, an "eschatological approach is intensely . . .," *Transforming Fate into Destiny,* 167.

Calmness and Equilibrium

Naomi Klein is quoted from her *The Shock Doctrine: The Rise of Disaster Capitalism* (New York: Metropolitan, 2007), 458.

Howard Thurman is quoted from his *Meditations of the Heart* (Boston: Beacon, 1981), 110. I am grateful to Debra Dean Murphy for drawing this reference to my attention.

Stanley Hauerwas is quoted from his *Christian Existence Today,* 256–57.

Joy

Barth, "Christ is risen . . .," *Church Dogmatics* III/4 (Edinburgh: T. & T. Clark, 1961), 375–76. For a beautiful account of the fundamental joyfulness of the Christian faith, grounded in Barth's theology, see Ralph C. Wood, *The Comedy of Redemption: Christian Faith and Comic Vision in Four American Novelists* (Notre Dame, IN: University of Notre Dame Press, 1988), 1–79.

Nietzsche is quoted from Barth, *Church Dogmatics* III/4, 377.

Barth, "To be joyful . . .," *Church Dogmatics* III/4, 378.

Barth, the one "who takes to heart . . .," *Church Dogmatics* III/4, 376.

Rutledge on Desmond Tutu's laugh, Rutledge, *The Crucifixion*, 124, note 40.

"Jesus is victor" was the motto of the nineteenth-century, father-and-son German pastors Johann Christoph Blumhardt and Christoph Friedrich Blumhardt. For their inspiring story and influence on Karl Barth, see Christian T. Collins Winn, *"Jesus Is Victor!": The Significance of the Blumhardts for the Theology of Karl Barth* (Eugene, OR: Pickwick, 2009). For excerpts from their writings, deeply rooted in an inaugurated and holistic eschatology, see ed. Vernard Eller, *Thy Kingdom Come: A Blumhardt Reader* (Grand Rapids: Eerdmans, 1980).

ACKNOWLEDGMENTS

I am happily indebted to friends who read this book in manuscript, provided encouragement, and saved me from mistakes. They include Stanley Hauerwas, Mother B. J. Heyboer, Richard Middleton, Dennis Okholm, Alan Padgett, and Scott Young. Whatever mistakes or infelicities remain belong only to me, for their careful readings significantly improved the book.

My wife, Sandy, has essentially supported me in the writing of all my books. She patiently endures extra solitary time as I retreat to the keyboard at all hours. She takes up the slack I then leave, fairly or not, in our home economics. She cheerfully hears my reports on progress or stasis in the creative process. In the case of this book, life with Sandy B. contributed immeasurably. Though I love creation, she has the greater facility for identifying flowers, trees, and birdsong. Her faithfully tended birdfeeders bring wildlife to our backyard. Her daily attention to weather makes her an amateur meteorologist of abiding fascination. She keeps this dreamer down to the earth that sustains us all. Truly, without her I could not be me, not least as a writer. So she is practically a coauthor, especially of chapter 6. My deepest and enduring love, Sand.

Given my angular personality, anomalous convictions, and anti-corporate intuitions, my editorial career has not always been without friction. But never have I been at home more than with than editors and other staff of Cascade Books. It is a constant joy and privilege to work with Jon Stock, Jimmy Stock, Jim Tedrick, K. C. Hanson, Robin Parry, Chris Spinks, Charlie Collier, and

Acknowledgments

others. My thanks especially to Charlie for his editorial shepherding of this book.